IARIA

SMART ACCESSIBILITY 2018

The Third International Conference on Universal Accessibility in the Internet of Things and Smart Environments

March 25 – 29, 2018

Rome, Italy

SMART ACCESSIBILITY 2018 Editors

Lukas Smirek, Stuttgart-Media University, Germany
Jon Sanford, Georgia Tech, USA
Steven Mannheimer, Indiana University, USA

Printed from e-media with permission by:

Curran Associates, Inc.
57 Morehouse Lane
Red Hook, NY 12571

Some format issues inherent in the e-media version may also appear in this print version.

Printed by Curran Associates, Inc. (2018)

International Academy, Research, and Industry Association (IARIA)
412 Derby Way
Wilmington, DE 19810

Phone: (408) 893-6407
Fax: (408) 527-6351

petre@iaria.org

Additional copies of this publication are available from:

Curran Associates, Inc.
57 Morehouse Lane
Red Hook, NY 12571 USA
Phone: 845-758-0400
Fax: 845-758-2633
Email: curran@proceedings.com
Web: www.proceedings.com

SMART ACCESSIBILITY 2018

Forward

The Third International Conference on Universal Accessibility in the Internet of Things and Smart Environments (SMART ACCESIBILITY 2018) was held in Rome, Italy, March 25 - 29, 2018

There are several similar definitions for universal accessibility, such as design for all, universal design, inclusive design, accessible design, and barrier free design. These and similar approaches are relevant to this conference. The focus will be on methods, tools, techniques and applications for human diversity, social inclusion and equality, enabling all people to have equal opportunities and to participate in the information society.

The accepted papers covered topics such as accessibility by design, digital inclusion, accessibility devices and applications. We believe that the SMART ACCESIBILITY 2018 contributions offered a large panel of solutions to key problems in areas of accessibility.

We take here the opportunity to warmly thank all the members of the SMART ACCESIBILITY 2018 technical program committee as well as the numerous reviewers. The creation of such a broad and high quality conference program would not have been possible without their involvement. We also kindly thank all the authors that dedicated much of their time and efforts to contribute to the SMART ACCESIBILITY 2018. We truly believe that thanks to all these efforts, the final conference program consists of top quality contributions.

This event could also not have been a reality without the support of many individuals, organizations and sponsors. In addition, we also gratefully thank the members of the SMART ACCESIBILITY 2018 organizing committee for their help in handling the logistics and for their work that is making this professional meeting a success.

We hope the SMART ACCESIBILITY 2018 was a successful international forum for the exchange of ideas and results between academia and industry and to promote further progress in the universal accessibility field.

We also hope that Nice provided a pleasant environment during the conference and everyone saved some time for exploring this beautiful city.

SMART ACCESIBILITY 2018 Chairs

Lukas Smirek, Stuttgart-Media University, Germany
Kristin Skeide Fuglerud, NR–Norsk Regnesentral, Norway
Christian Bühler, University of Dortmund, Germany

Daniela Marghitu, Auburn University - Auburn, USA
Simeon Keates, University of Greenwich, UK

SMART ACCESSIBILITY 2018

COMMITTEE

Copyright Information

Table of Contents

Audio Guided Driving for People with Blindness with Seated Self-balancing Personal Transporters 1
Andreas Hub and Jutta Cook

Haptic Guided Driving with Seated Self-balancing Personal Transporters for People with Deafblindness 5
Andreas Hub and Jutta Cook

Trusted Mobile Zone Solution Based on Virtualization Technology 10
GeonLyang Kim and JeongNyeo Kim

Utility of a Mobile Route Planning App for People Aging with Disability 12
Jon A. Sanford, Subhrajit Guhathakurta, Sarah Melgen, and Ge Zhang

A Qualitative Approach to Understanding User Needs for Aging with Disability 18
Elena T. Remillard, Tracy L. Mitzner, Jenny L. Singleton, and Wendy A. Rogers

Design Criteria to Advance Technologies for the Aging Population 23
Claudia Rebola

Universally Designed mHealth App for Individuals Aging with Multiple Sclerosis 29
Ljilja Ruzic, Harshal P. Mahajan, and Jon A. Sanford

Effects of Advanced Driver Assistance System for Elderly's Safe Transportation 36
Ryosuke Ando, Yasuhiro Mimura, Yasuhide Nishihori, and Jia Yang

The Role of the Internet and Technology in the Wellbeing of People with Physical Disabilities 42
Alexandra Young, Tom Dening, and Chris Greenhalgh

TELEPROM-G: A Study Evaluating Access and Care Delivery of Telehealth Services among Community-Based Seniors with Depressive Symptoms 45
Cheryl Forchuk, Akshya Vasudev, Amer Burhan, Puneet Seth, and Tony O'Regan

SAMIoT – Middleware based on IoT for Irrigation Planning on Large-scale Crops 51
Hugo Ordonez, Jose Luis Rivas, Juliana Sanchez, Javier Carbonell, Edgar HIncapie, and Armando Ordonez

Experimental Study on Riding Skill for Using Standing Type Vehicles 60
Naohisa Hashimoto, Jyeon Kim, Kohji Tomita, Simon Thompson, Yusuke Takinami, and Osamu Matsumoto

Towards Smart Public Transport Data 66
Paloma Caceres Garcia de Marina, Almudena Sierra Alonso, Belen Vela Sanchez, Jose Maria Cavero Barca, and Carlos Enrique Cuesta Quintero

Audio Guided Driving for People with Blindness with Seated Self-balancing Personal Transporters

Andreas Hub
BNI Blindnavigation International gGmbH
Ayestr. 2
88441 Mittelbiberach, Germany
e-mail: andreas.hub@blindnavigation.org

Jutta Cook
CO_4 Communications
Talfeldstr.10
88400 Biberach, Germany
e-mail: jutta.cook@co4-communications.com

***Abstract*—This paper presents a new approach to increase the range of mobility for people with blindness or severe visual impairments, while enhancing interaction-driven accessibility with sighted people. For the blind or visually impaired, covering longer distances often poses a special challenge; prolonged use of a cane or leaning on a sighted person can be exhausting and can lead to unhealthy and non-ergonomic motions. Guided use of a modified seated, self-balanced single person vehicle enhances accessibility of various environments, serves as physical training, offers great experiences and fosters both self-esteem and independence – thus serving as a catalyst for positive changes in many different aspects of life. Moving together constitutes implicit social interaction and social participation. In this paper, we describe the practical implementation and address challenges concerning the blind drivers' perception of velocity and direction of movement. We expect these challenges to be solved in the near future through the application of either existing or new haptic devices. Our tests with persons having visual, other sensory, or mobility impairments show that they are perfectly capable of driving an AddSeat®, which contributed to significantly increasing accessible environments, enhanced their mobility, expanded their social interaction, increased their physical fitness and greatly improved their general outlook on life.**

Keywords-Interaction-driven accessibility; visual impairments; self-balancing personal transporter; physical therapy training.

I. Introduction

For people with blindness, it is often a special challenge to cover longer distances. A prolonged use of a cane can be exhausting for the muscles in the hand, arm and shoulder. Walking alongside a sighted person for longer periods of time can be stressful, too, for people with visual impairments. Both can lead to unhealthy and non-ergonomic motions, causing muscle sores, cramps and other discomfort in the musculoskeletal system. Another aspect is that many people with sensory deficits have difficulties or are (for good reasons) afraid of using personal single seat vehicles developed for sighted drivers, such as bicycles, motor bikes or others, such as the Segway® PT (Personal Transporter) [1] that are operated in a standing position.

For a number of years, there has been ongoing research as summarized, e.g., by Mandel in [2] and there is an array of products on the market with a more or less implicit aim of autonomous driving for wheelchair users.

Figure 1. The picture shows a blind AddSeat® driver in an indoor environment.

In contrast to these projects, our study focused on the idea of letting blind people drive on their own as much as possible and be in charge of the device. We assumed that this in particular provides a feeling of freedom and independence, especially when the additional hints given by a sighted guide could be kept to a minimum.

For a few years, there have been several special wheelchairs on the market with only two wheels based on Segway® PT self-balancing technologies, such as a model named Genny Urban 2.0L and one named Freee F2, both available from Urban Mobility 24 [3][4].

Swedish manufacturer AddMovement [5] has one seated, single person vehicle also based on a Segway® PT, which we deemed suitable for this study. Their so-called AddSeat® comes equipped with a panic-braking mechanism that can be easily triggered by moving the seat glider backwards – a feature we thought useful as it compensates for the time-laps between the advice given by the guide and the actual reaction of the blind driver.

For our tests, we used an AddSeat® based on a Segway® PT i2 suitable for indoor environments (Figure 1) as well as outdoors (Figure 2).

Figure 2. The photo depicts one of our blind test persons outdoors in a full stop emergency brake action.

The dimensions of this model are quite narrow, making it hardly any wider than the shoulders of our drivers. This allows for access to any standard elevator. In addition, the AddSeat can turn on the spot as it only has one axle and does not need the additional front wheels of a conventional wheelchair. In outdoor tests with sighted people, it could be shown that the AddSeat® is suitable for gradual inclines as well as demanding ground conditions such as gravel, grass or even firm sand. The vehicle also mastered snowy spots where maneuvering a conventional wheelchair would be challenging. In tests with people with mobility impairments (amputations, paraplegia, autoimmune disorders, etc.) seated self-balancing transporters have already been proven to be a life-changing addition. Customers reported a tremendous increase in quality of life as it enhanced their mobility and independence, it opened up their social range of motion and allowed them to take on completely new roles within their family lives. The changes included self-determined shopping tours, and taking on considerably more responsibility for others, e.g., own young children or domestic animals [6][7].

With these great gains in mind, the question was, if those could also be transferred to people with visual impairments.

The rest of this paper is structured as follows. Section II describes the technical features of the AddSeat® and its benefits for daily life. We also explain the briefing method used for our test persons. Section III describes the resulting feedback from our test drivers as well as possible implications. In section IV, we conclude with lessons learned and suggestions for future work, including desirable technical adaptions and how to enhance the enforcement of the rights of persons with disabilities.

II. Methods

Device: Driving an AddSeat® is quite simple and intuitive. For our tests, we used an AddSeat® model 5.1, equipped with a seat featuring pneumatic suspension and height adjustment. Those features bring a range of advantages. For one, it is more comfortable than a model with a fixed seat. Secondly, the user can raise the seat to a height that allows communication with standing people almost at eye level (depending on the person's height).

Sighted Addseat® drivers told us the elevated position also reduces or annihilates the claustrophobic feelings they often experience in crowds, when all they get to see in a regular lower wheelchair is the less attractive middle part of others' bodies. This feature is not only comfortable for both sides during talks, it also changes perception as it literally raises both partners onto the same level and thereby avoids the unpleasant feeling of being talked down to many people with all kinds of handicaps have to experience on a daily basis.

Handling: With both parking brakes on, the user places himself on the AddSeat®. Then the parking handles on the right and left side have to be released. Now, the PT is in balance mode and the user can start driving. A forward motion is achieved by moving the upper part of the body forward, backwards correspondingly. The underlying technical principle is a shift in the center of gravity. The AddSeat®'s seat is mounted on a sliding rail, enabling the driver to very rapidly shift his center of mass. A quick backwards or forwards shift allows the driver to perform very precise driving motions, such as needed in order to avoid moving obstacles. The quick backwards shift can also be used to rapidly stop the vehicle in an effective full stop emergency brake maneuver. This use of a sliding mechanism can reduce the braking distance by several meters, especially when moving at velocities greater than 10 km/h. For blind drivers, reconnaissance of moving obstacles or other people and animals definitely requires a sighted person to move along and advise appropriately, especially at higher speeds.

Our two blind test persons – one adult woman and one adult man – first received a short introduction to the functionality of the AddSeat®. Both test persons were working for several years as consultants, providing advice on medical aids to people with visual impairments. We knew of both being physically active and having good body tension. Therefore, we expected both to be able to steer the AddSeat® with controlled movements of the upper part of their bodies. In fact, we realized very quickly that they performed much better than some sighted subjects, even without visual feedback. Both drivers quickly grasped how to move forward and backward, how to navigate turns and how to stop using the gliding seat. They intuitively were able to turn in place, e.g., within a narrow elevator. This brief driving lesson only took a few minutes and in principle enabled our blind test drivers to handle the vehicle by themselves. During those explanations, haptic support was used to provide principle movement and velocity information as well as direction suggestions. For this, we used a haptic training method comparable to Riitta Lathinen's haptices and haptemes advices [8]. This method of very short haptic signs was originally developed to provide complex information such as room structures within seconds, using the surface of body parts of people with deafblindness. We adapted this method for navigation purposes. The role of the sighted guide was then to give either acoustical hints such as "more left or right" or "slower and faster" or to provide this kind of short haptic navigation advices. To enhance the forward movement, the sighted guide gave a gentle tap on the driver's upper back until the velocity was appropriate with respect to the environment and the driver's capacities. To trigger a left or a right turn, a finger tap was given on the corresponding shoulder. Braking or velocity reduction were induced by a softer and longer tip with the finger or hand on the front of the driver's shoulder.

After this "haptic" driving lesson, further minimal driving hints were provided acoustically by the sighted guide – comparable to guided alpine or cross-country skiing. We consider this to be the preferred guiding method as long as there are no hearing problems or noisy environments.

III. Results

Both blind drivers learned to understand, to steer and to control the AddSeat® within a few minutes. Bigger challenges arose for the sighted guides, who had to keep up and provide adequate and precise acoustical navigation advice.

As part of the results we would like to cite one of our blind test drivers (A.K.): "At the exhibition "RehaCare" in Düsseldorf, I had the great possibility to take a ride on the AddSeat.

First, I had to find out how to really get myself positioned on the seat and that I could easily determine directions by moving my body forward, backward and to the sides. The first motions were a little bit shaky, but once I got used to the AddSeat and learned how to control it, riding became more and more fun. After a short while, I got a good feeling on how to move backward and forward and how to slow down or to speed up. After we moved around through the halls for a while, we went outside and I could ride the Add-Seat in "open-air". I enjoyed moving through the crowd, listening to the noises around me. In addition, it was a warm, lovely afternoon. Much too soon, the ride was over and we had to get back to the booth where we had started off. In a nutshell: I enjoyed this experience a lot and would do it again any time." The statement of the second person (S.P.) was quite similar with regard to contents.

Both blind test persons reported that it was not always clear for them whether they were driving forward or backward as they were missing visual input, in particular when moving slowly. For the same reason they reported difficulties estimating their current velocity.

Although blind use of an AddSeat® is not completely without risks, the atmosphere during the tests was very relaxed. And it turned out that joining in this new type of sports activity offered pure fun for the test drivers as well as for the sighted guides. While guided skiing can only be done in special places and when snow is available, guided driving with AddSeats® does not have those restrictions. It can generally be performed anywhere at any given time.

The results from additional test drives and discussions with other blind people about seated self-balancing personal transporters were that these vehicles can and will have many more implications aside from fun and sporting activities. We include these implications in the following section.

IV. Conclusion and Future Work

The idea of letting blind people by themselves handle a vehicle that can travel up to 20 km/h might at first glance look somewhat dangerous. And many people with sensory deficits have difficulties or are afraid of using personal single seat vehicles developed for sighted drivers, such as bicycles, motor bikes or vehicles operated in a standing position like a regular Segway® PT.

On the other hand, blind skiers proved able to reach amazing speeds beyond 100 km/h. In our study, it was not our aim to determine how fast one can go or to look into legal aspects such as registration, liability insurance or restrictions to access in different places. Our main focus was: can persons with blindness or visual impairments safely maneuver an AddSeat®, and what positive implications do they stand to gain?

During our test drives we learned:

- Driving an AddSeat® is not without risks (which might be the nature of many things fun) – in particular when driving with visual impairments or blind.
- Under the pre-condition of good control over the upper part of their body, driving an AddSeat® can greatly enhance the quality of life for the blind as well as people with visual impairments.
- Steering an AddSeat® is sport and good physio, as it provides training for a better control of the upper body in an ergonomic position by supporting improvements of the abdominal and back muscles.
- Even drivers lacking physical fitness are able to cover long distances in a healthier position for the upper part of their body, compared to conventional wheelchairs. The range of an AddSeat® can extend 30 km depending on several factors such as wind speed and direction, the driver's weight, the contour of the terrain or the traction of the wheels. This greatly enhances the radius self-determined and largely independent movement for the driver.
- We are sure that audio pilot systems used in blind alpine skiing can significantly enhance the quality of navigation advices as well as allow for better and more regular conversation between the blind driver and the guide.
- From our tests with sighted people with mobility restrictions, we established the large influence of the AddSeat® on the aspects of life we differentiated as "fun", "freedom" and "family & friends", resulting in a more self-determined, independent, non-discriminated and equitable life. We do not see any reasons why those results should not apply to blind people. However, we recommend that blind people drive only with an experienced guide – perhaps on a second vehicle in order to keep up – especially in challenging environments such country lanes, steep roads etc., and most certainly at higher speeds.

- After all our experience concerning navigation support for people with blindness and deafblindness [9]-[11], there is no doubt that quite a number of them will be able to profit from driving AddSeat®. However, people with complete deafblindness will benefit strongly from additional interfaces to interact with the sighted guide. One option would be to use slightly modified systems, such as the NavBelt [13]. Alternatively, other additional handheld devices offering adaptive control elements and a haptic compass could be applied [14].
- Guided AddSeat® driving might be the basis for important additional social interactions as well as a healthy, ergonomic way of moving also for people with multiple mobility restrictions concerning sensory and/or physical aspects.

FUTURE WORK: To solve the issues of missing information for blind drivers concerning current position, movement direction, orientation and velocity, we implemented human advice. In the future, we suggest to standardize acoustical or haptic advices or the use of additional technical support. So far, we identified two possibilities. One: Haptic devices to be either carried on the driver's body or mounted to the AddSeat®'s seat or steering bar. The other option would be the implementation of autonomous driving systems used in cars or other wheelchairs with four wheels. During our experiments however, we gained the impression that our test persons appreciated the self-determination and independence coming with being in control of the machine.

Future work should also include the question, if the AddSeat® can be used to support more people with visual impairments and different degrees of restrictions. More research should be conducted to determine whether the positive effects of using an AddSeat® can be translated into other aspects of life, such as the workplace. Maybe it is possible to create new kinds of workplaces or make existing employment opportunities accessible for these groups of people.

Lastly, one of the major stumbling blocks also needs to be addressed in the near future: the question under which legal conditions and/or training requirements the blind driver and the guide are allowed to drive on public streets in different countries. Our tests have shown that suitable, hearing test persons were able to steer seated personal transporters indoors and outdoors with a high degree of precision, supported by a sighted guide. The United Nations' Convention on the Rights of Persons with Disabilities [15] requires all parties to support technologies and solutions affording persons with disabilities include the rights to accessibility, the rights to live independently and be included in the community (Article 19), to personal mobility (article 20), habilitation and rehabilitation (Article 26), and to participation in political, public, and cultural life as well as recreation and sport (Articles 29 and 30). Therefore, rules and regulations on a national, regional and local level should be amended in order to allow for blind people to operate such vehicles in combination with a guide.

ACKNOWLEDGMENT

We would like thank our test drivers Anne Kochanek and Sascha Paul. Additionally, we would like to thank Mike Redford with AddMovement AB for providing us with the test vehicle for this research experiments.

REFERENCES

[1] http://www.segway.com/ 2018.03.07

[2] C. Mandel. Navigation of the Smart Wheelchair Rolland. Kumulative Dissertation, 2007.

[3] http://www.urbanmobility24.de/genny.html 2018.01.31

[4] http://www.urbanmobility24.de/Freee.html 2018.01.31

[5] http://addmovement.com/ 2018.03.07

[6] http://addmovement.com/customervideos.html 2018.01.31

[7] http://addmovement.com/AddMvideos.html 2018.01.31

[8] R. Lahtinen. Haptices and haptemes. A case study of developmental process in touch-based communication of acquired deafblind people. PhD thesis, 2008.

[9] A. Hub, J. Diepstraten and T. Ertl, "Design and development of an indoor navigation and object identification system for the blind" Assets '04: Proceedings of the 6th international ACM SIGACCESS conference on Computers and accessibility, pp. 147-152, 2004.

[10] A. Hub, "Map Requirements and Attainable Public Policy for an Installation-free Worldwide Navigation and Information System for the Blind" In: Proceedings of the 9th International Conference on Low Vision (Vision 2008), July 7-11 Montreal, Canada, 2008. [Online]. Available from: http://citeseerx.ist.psu.edu/viewdoc/download?doi=10.1.1.230.927&rep=rep1&type=pdf 2018.02.04

[11] A. Hub, "Integration of Active Tactile Control Braille Technology into Portable Navigation and Object Recognition Systems for the Blind and Deafblind" In: Proceedings of the 9th International Conference on Low Vision (Vision 2008), July 7-11 Montreal, Canada, 2008. [Online]. Available from: ftp://ftp.informatik.uni-stuttgart.de/pub/library/ncstrl.ustuttgart_fi/INPROC-2008-128/INPROC-2008-128.pdf 2018.01.01

[12] A. Hub, "Guiding Grids in Augmented Maps for Precise Installation-Free Worldwide Blind Navigation" In: Proceedings of the California State University Northridge Center on Disabilities' 23rd Annual International Technology and Persons with Disabilities Conference (CSUN 2008), March 10-15, Los Angeles, CA, USA, 2008. [Online]. Available from: http://citeseerx.ist.psu.edu/viewdoc/download?doi=10.1.1.230.1905&rep=rep1&type=pdf 2018.02.04

[13] J. Borenstein, "The NavBelt - A Computerized Multi-Sensor Travel Aid for Active Guidance of the Blind" In: Proceedings of the CSUN's Fifth Annual Conference on Technology and Persons with Disabilities, Los Angeles, California, March 21-24, pp. 107-116, 1990.

[14] J. Winterholler and B. Janny, "Innovative Haptic Interface for Navigation" In: Proceedings of the California State University Northridge Center on Disabilities 28th Annual International Technology and Persons with Disabilities Conference (CSUN 2013), February 25 - March 2, San Diego, CA, USA, 2013. [Online]. Available from: http://www.csun.edu/cod/conference/2013/sessions/index.php/public/presentations/view/130 2018.02.01

[15] United Nations. Convention on the Rights of Persons with Disabilities. [Online]. Available from: http://www.un.org/disabilities/documents/convention/convoptprot-e.pdf 2018.01.30

Haptic Guided Driving with Seated Self-balancing Personal Transporters for People with Deafblindness

Andreas Hub
BNI Blindnavigation International gGmbH
Ayestr. 2
88441 Mittelbiberach, Germany
e-mail: andreas.hub@blindnavigation.org

Jutta Cook
CO_4 Communications
Talfeldstr.10
88400 Biberach, Germany
e-mail: jutta.cook@co4-communications.com

Abstract—**In this paper, we will present the experiences from our work in progress with a first test drive with a new seated self-balancing personal transporter by an entirely deafblind driver, supported by a guide. Our aim is to help reduce the feeling of isolation and dependency and the restrictions in the range of mobility deafblind people report. Using this personal transporter greatly enlarges the distance a deafblind person can cover in a self-determined way. Being active and moving together constitutes significant, essential social interaction and social participation. It offers a very relaxed atmosphere of independence while fostering a relationship of mutual trust. Within this paper, we describe how it works and also some challenges concerning the deafblind driver's feelings about missing visual information such as the position, the driving direction and the current velocity. These challenges might be solved in the near future by using additional existing or new haptic devices. We are confident that, this way, we could make significantly enlarged environments accessible in a smart way for people with deafblindness as well as for people with additional physical restrictions.**

Keywords-accessibility; deafblindess; mobility; haptics; self-balancing personal transporter.

I. INTRODUCTION

For years, there have been numerous research projects, e.g., the Rolland project [1], as well as a number of quite sophisticated products on the market, enabling drivers to use electronic wheelchairs autonomously or with only a minimum of motoric input, such as eye trackers, minimal joysticks or other control mechanisms that can be operated, e.g., with only one finger or a small head motion.

In contrast to these wheelchairs, the self-balancing personal transporter we used demands real physical activity from its driver. The so called AddSeat® by Swedish manufacturer AddMovement [2] is a self-balancing seated single person vehicle based on a Segway® Personal Transporter (PT). It was initially developed to enable people with physical mobility restrictions such as amputations, paraplegia, autoimmune disorders, etc. to move around more self-determined than in a regular electric wheelchair.

In field reports and video documentations, we were able to show that driving a seated self-balancing Personal Transporter for several weeks can significantly increase the independence and quality of life. This includes feelings of joy and fun brought on by experiencing the physical sensations of movement. This is also applied in challenging environments such as trails, grass, snow, or sand where it would be difficult or impossible to maneuver with other types of wheelchairs (Figure 1).

Figure 1. Successful tests with sighted people with other mobility restrictions (in this case a high leg amputation) were the motivation to expand these tests to guided driving with a deafblind person.

People with complete deafblindness rarely have an opportunity to feel the physical forces that come with driving a motor-powered vehicle on their own, such as acceleration or centripetal forces, including the fun and the feeling of freedom that can be related with driving faster. However, from our previous work concerning navigation support for people with deafblindness [3]-[7], we know some of their dreams of freedom and independence concern mobility, including the wish to drive extremely fast vehicles, such as motorbikes even Jet Skis®. Especially in cases where deafblindness occurs only later in life, people might already have gained the experience of driving, and really want to do it again. With this background in mind, we established the idea of letting a first, suitable deafblind test person drive an AddSeat® (Figure 2).

Figure 2. The photo shows the test driver on the vehicle, receiving a short briefing on how to steer the AddSeat® sighted guide using Lorm fingerspelling.

Good posture and control of the upper body is the main pre-condition to being able to steer an AddSeat® in a controlled manner. This applies to sighted drivers, too. According to our experience, some people with complete deafblindness have very good posture and body control even though they are lacking visual or acoustical input, which makes visual or acoustical corrections of malposition impossible.

In prior tests with people with mobility impairments, the AddSeat® technology has already proven to be a life-changing addition [8]. Participants reported a tremendous increase in quality of life as it enhanced their mobility and independence, it opened up their social range of motion and allowed them to take on completely new roles within their family lives. Additionally, it turned out that people without mobility restrictions can benefit from this vehicle, too. The AddSeat® can cover distances beyond 30 km. Its big wheels and good traction even make decent slopes, farming roads or broader trails in the mountains accessible. We see a special benefit in this way of locomotion for people with visual impairments, as a prolonged use of a cane can be exhausting for the muscles in the hand, arm and shoulder. Walking alongside a sighted person for longer periods of time can be stressful, too. Both can lead to unhealthy and non-ergonomic motions, causing muscle sores, cramps and other discomforts in the musculoskeletal system.

During prior experiments with blind AddSeat® drivers, we saw that their abilities to control both their bodies and the vehicle often surmounted those of sighted subjects. In comparison to persons with deafblindness, blind people have the advantage of being able to estimate their current position, direction, and velocity by using acoustical input; they either use noises in the environment or produce sounds of their own, as a click of the tongue, singing, talking or knocking the cane on the floor, etc. The acoustic response of those sounds helps them to detect environmental structures, such as open doors, and to estimate their own velocity or the velocity of others, such as the Doppler frequency shift of cars near crosswalks. People with complete deafblindness are void of this kind of sensory input. With both visual and hearing senses missing, their sense of gravity and appertaining their sense of body control plays a more important role than in people without sensory restrictions.

Structure of this paper: Section II describes the technical features of the AddSeat® and the methods we used for the briefing the deafblind person as well as for the driving support provided by the sighted guide. Section III describes the results concerning the astonishing feasibility of the principle, but it also addresses the remaining challenges concerning mainly technical issues such as hardware integration. In Section IV, we conclude this early stage of our investigations and suggest a compass for the future work in this new field of research for people with deafblindness.

II. Methods

Driving an AddSeat® is quite simple and intuitive. The AddSeat® is the only self-balancing vehicle available on the market that is equipped with a panic-braking mechanism, so far. For our tests, we used an AddSeat® model 5.1 equipped with pneumatic suspension and height adjustment. We deemed those features essential in testing seated Segways® with a deafblind person supported by a sighted guide. Those features bring a range of advantages for sighted people, too. For one, it is more comfortable than a model with a fixed seat. Secondly, the user can raise the seat to allow communication at almost eye level with others standing, depending on the person's height. This feature is not only comfortable for both sides, but being at eye level also greatly changes people's perception.

The first thing the driver has to do is to place himself on the AddSeat®. Next, the parking handles on both sides have to be released. Now, the vehicle is in balance mode and the user can drive forward by moving the upper part of the body forward or correspondingly backward by shifting the center of gravity to the rear. The seat of the AddSeat® is mounted on a sliding rail. Thus, the driver can very rapidly shift his center of mass. A quick backwards or forwards shift allows the driver to perform precise driving maneuvers such as avoiding moving obstacles. It can also be used to quickly stop the vehicle in an effective full stop emergency brake maneuver. Implementation of this sliding mechanism reduced the braking distance by several meters, in particular when driving at speeds exceeding 10 km/h. In order to avoid collisions with moving obstacles or other people, it was necessary to have a sighted person walk along and advise appropriately.

Our deafblind male driver received a short briefing from a sighted guide by using Lorm fingerspelling [9]. He quickly grasped how to move forward and backward, how to navigate turns and how to stop by using the gliding seat. He intuitively was able to turn in place. This brief driving lesson only took a few minutes and in principle enabled the deafblind test driver to handle the vehicle by himself. During this short driving lesson, haptic support was used to provide

Figure 3. The photo depicts the sighted guide standing behind the driver, giving him the haptic sign for driving straight ahead with the same velocity by moving the back of the hand up and down the driver's spine.

Figure 4. This picture shows how finger tapping on the by the corresponding shoulder was used as haptic sign for left and right turns.

principle movement and velocity information as well as direction suggestions. For this, we used a haptic training method comparable to Riitta Lathinen's haptices and haptemes advices [10]. To enhance the forward movement, the sighted guide gave a gentle tap on the driver's upper back until the velocity was appropriate with respect to the environment and the driver's capacities (Figure 3). To trigger a left or a right turn, a finger or hand tap was given on the corresponding shoulder (Figure 4). Braking or velocity reduction were induced by a softer and longer tip with the finger or hand on the front of the driver's shoulder. For safety reasons, we had a third person chaperone every test in the background as to minimize risks in the initial phase of the test.

III. RESULTS

The deafblind test driver learned to understand, to steer and to control the AddSeat® within a few minutes. The challenge for the sighted guide was to provide adequate and precise navigation advices using haptic commands.

As part of the results we would like to cite our deafblind test driver (P.H.) (information in [..] was shown in signs): "It's a pity that I can't see a little. Otherwise I would start immediately to drive around. My biggest problem is to be completely blind. I can well imagine that people with limited visual impairments can use it [quite easy]. It's also possible [for me] to feel safe [because it's stable to the side]. To help with orientation for [completely] blind people, we need something additional." In addition, he reported that it was not always clear for him whether he was driving forward or backward, in particular when driving slowly, as he was missing all visual or acoustical input. For the same reason, he reported difficulties estimating his current velocity. The used haptic and direct type of driving advice offers the advantage that it can be translated into action a lot more intuitively and faster than conventional sign language or fingerspelling.

IV. CONCLUSION

Our main focus was on feasibility – can a deafblind person steer a single seat personal transporter – and what are the emotional and social effects associated with moving self-determined at greater speeds. We have reached a couple of conclusions.

The physical task of steering the AddSeat® is mainly a matter of upper body control which we found not to be negatively influenced by the co-occurrence of visual and acoustic impairments. Our deafblind test person performed better than some sighted testers, a fact we attribute to his heightened sense for posture and position. However, we have to say that we picked our deafblind test person based on the precondition of a good general mobility as to make successful testing more probable.

After a quick instruction session with haptic translation, our test person was able to steer the vehicle by himself with the help of a very limited set of haptic guidance signs such as left, right, forward, back or keeping a steady pace. We conclude that these basic instructions could also be given by a sighted guide lacking knowledge of Lorm language, thereby potentially widening the circle of interactive contacts a deafblind person can have. Guided driving on an AddSeat® might therefore be the basis for an increase in important social interaction.

Our previous tests with sighted people with mobility restrictions showed the AddSeat®'s significant positive influence on more than mobility. Three dimensions of life which we labeled "fun", "freedom" and "family&friends" yielded especially positive results: self-determined driving enabled those test persons to be more independent and lead a more equitable life with less discrimination. It can be reasonably assumed that driving an AddSeat® can also enhance the quality of life for people with deafblindness, as well as for their partners, family members, friends and caregivers.

Driving an AddSeat® is not without risks, in particular when driving deafblind. We strongly recommend that deafblind people drive only with an experienced guide, especially in challenging environments such country lanes, steep roads etc. and most certainly at higher speeds. Deafblind drivers will need a way of receiving constant advice while moving. The relationship between the driver and the sighted guide is one of extreme mutual trust, as the driver lays his well-being and ultimately his life into the hands of his guide. The sighted person in return takes over the responsibility of safeguarding his guidee, relying on him to perform the required actions. This can be a great step towards breaking the isolation.

With its range of up to 30 km, the AddSeat® lets drivers cover long distances. Its off-road capabilities make a wide array of different environments accessible to deafblind people. As the AddSeat®'s movement is controlled by shifting the driver's center of gravity, every change of speed or direction also serves as a work-out to improve the abdominal and back muscles.

FUTURE WORK:

This work is at an early stage. The next step will be to increase the number of usability tests while establishing a questionnaire that allows for an evaluation of a wider range of variables. We also suggest a comparison between sighted, blind, and deafblind drivers as well as design options for the haptic feedback device that could then be utilized for all groups.

After our research experience concerning object recognition and navigation support for people with deafblindness, there is no doubt that quite a number of them will be able to profit from driving an AddSeat®. People with complete deafblindness will have the best experiences with additional support from haptic interfaces implemented to interact with the sighted guide or by driving completely autonomous – conceivably through the integration of autonomous driving systems used in the car industry or in electronic wheelchairs with four wheels. Those systems, however, might imply that in the future the driver has nothing to do at all while driving. All our tests, also with sighted people, have shown that the drivers actually enjoy the very act of driving; driving alone or together with a guide is fun, because they get to perform the task themselves. It is this activity that sets driving an AddSeat® apart from their usual, passive experience of being taken somewhere. We gained the impression that this is particularly the case with blind users as well as with our deafblind tester, too. Therefore, we decided to focus our future work on ideas for systems that allow the driver to keep in control of the steering rod and the motor power, with navigation support from a sighted guide through a haptic interface. Here, future research can look into two different options. One is to have a haptic assistance system controlled by the guide attached directly onto the driver's body. The other possibility is to integrate the haptic interface onto or into the AddSeat®. An example of a body-fixed system that might be used with slight modifications in combination with the AddSeat® is the NavBelt [11]. It provides acoustic information and additional vibrating haptic information within a belt around the body. This system could be particularly helpful concerning direction advices from the guide. The NavBelt has the advantage that the driver keeps both hands free to steer the AddSeat® more safely than with just one hand.

Our previous research proposed alternative systems which are more or less handheld, such as the following: A portable Braille display connected to a smartphone with a special navigation software provides technical orientation support for people with blindness and deafblindness as developed in previous work [12]. This system uses short Braille patterns of two or three Braille characters, some of them animated, to indicate for example a right or a left turn. By using such short navigation advices, the blind user can be informed about the appropriate direction and speed faster than with complete written text information in Braille. The other proposed functional system [13] uses a haptic phone keyboard as basic user interface and applies additional adaptive control elements including a haptic compass. This allows the user to feel the direction of motion and to determine the current mode of the system without asking for it or without changing to another level in the program hierarchy. The advantage of this system is that it can be used as a compass-based navigation system.

When looking at future systems that might be fixed somehow to or on the AddSeat, we first think about slightly modified systems such as "The ViibraCane" based on the remote control of a Wii® game console proposed by Schmitz [14] that could be integrated into the handles of the steering rod. Another possibility would be to integrate vibrating or tactile elements into the seat to enhance the navigation support and to shorten reaction time similar to systems used in fighter jets [15][16]. Those kind of systems will be able to solve the challenges of missing information on current position, movement, direction and orientation for deafblind drivers. Future work should furthermore include the question if the AddSeat® can be used to support deafblind – with varying degrees of restrictions – in other fields, such as the workplace, or if it might be possible to create new kinds of workplaces for this group of people still experiencing discrimination in many aspects of life.

Finally, in the near future the question needs to be addressed how the requirements of the United Nations' Convention on the Rights of Persons with Disabilities [17] can be implemented by all parties to the convention on a national, regional and local level in order to afford deafblind people the right to participate in traffic with support from a sighted guide in order to benefit from this innovative and interactive technology. The sighted guide would need a secure command over only a very limited number of tactile gestures. This could be the basis for a sustainable way of "breaking the isolation", as it would multiply the number of potential communication partners usually limited by knowledge of complex languages with tactile signs. Even if this interaction would first pertain to navigation support only, it can still make all the difference for everybody involved.

ACKNOWLEDGMENT

We would like thank our test driver Peter Hepp and Margherita Hepp for the sign language interpretation, the fingerspelling and for being a perfect guide from the very beginning.

REFERENCES

[1] C. Mandel, Navigation of the Smart Wheelchair Rolland. Kumulative Dissertation, 2007.

[2] http://www.addmovement.com/ 2018.01.30

[3] A. Hub, J. Diepstraten, and T. Ertl, "Design of an Object Identification and Orientation Assistant for the Deafblind" In: Proceedings of the 6th DbI European Conference on Deafblindness, August 2-7, Presov, Slowakia, p. 97, 2005.

[4] A. Hub, S. Kombrink, K. Bosse, and T. Ertl, "Conference Navigation and Communication Assistant for the Deafblind based on Tactile and Acoustically Amplified Augmented Map Information for the 14th Deafblind International World Conference" In: Proceedings of the 14th Deafblind International World Conference (DbI 2007), September 25-30, Perth, Australia, 2007. [Online]. Available from: ftp://ftp.informatik.uni-stuttgart.de/pub/library/ncstrl.ustuttgart_fi/INPROC-2007-124/INPROC-2007-124.pdf 2018.02.01

[5] A. Hub, "Integration of Active Tactile Control Braille Technology into Portable Navigation and Object Recognition Systems for the Blind and Deafblind" In: Proceedings of the 9th International Conference on Low Vision (Vision 2008), July 7-11, Montreal, Canada, 2008. [Online]. Available from: ftp://ftp.informatik.uni-stuttgart.de/pub/library/ncstrl.ustuttgart_fi/INPROC-2008-128/INPROC-2008-128.pdf 2018.01.01

[6] A. Hub, "Making Complex Environments Accessible on the Basis of TANIA's Augmented Navigation Support" In: Proceedings of the California State University Northridge Center on Disabilities 25th Annual International Technology and Persons with Disabilities Conference (CSUN 2010), March 22-27, San Diego, CA, USA, 2010. [Online]. Available from: https://www.researchgate.net/publication/266282306_Making_Complex_Environments_Accessible_on_the_Basis_of_TANIA%27s_Augmented_Navigation_Support 2018.02.01

[7] A. Hub, Beyond the senses: model-based assistance systems for people with audio-visual impairments. Weiter als die Sinne reichen: Modellbasierte Assistenzsysteme für Menschen mit Hörsehschädigungen. In: Ursula Horsch, Andrea Wanka: Das Usher-Syndrom: Ein Fachbuch für Mediziner, Pädagogen, Psychologen und Betroffene. Reinhardt-Verlag, pp. 165-174, 2012.

[8] http://addmovement.com/video's.html 2018.03.08

[9] http://www.deafblind.com/lorm.html 2018.03.08

[10] R. Lahtinen, Haptices and haptemes. A case study of developmental process in touch-based communication of acquired deafblind people. PhD thesis, 2008.

[11] J. Borenstein, "The NavBelt - A Computerized Multi-Sensor Travel Aid for Active Guidance of the Blind" In: Proceedings of the CSUN's Fifth Annual Conference on Technology and Persons with Disabilities, Los Angeles, California, March 21-24, pp. 107-116, 1990.

[12] A. Hub, S. Krysmanski, "Navigation with Haptic or Braille Support" In: Proceedings of the California State University Northridge Center on Disabilities 28th Annual International Technology and Persons with Disabilities Conference (CSUN 2013), February 25 - March 2, San Diego, CA, USA, 2013. [Online]. Available from: http://www.csun.edu/cod/conference/2013/sessions/index.php/public/presentations/view/214 2018.02.01

[13] J. Winterholler and B. Janny, "Innovative Haptic Interface for Navigation" In: Proceedings of the California State University Northridge Center on Disabilities 28th Annual International Technology and Persons with Disabilities Conference (CSUN 2013), February 25 - March 2, San Diego, CA, USA, 2013. [Online]. Available from: http://www.csun.edu/cod/conference/2013/sessions/index.php/public/presentations/view/130 2018.02.01

[14] B. Schmitz, "The ViibraCane – A White Cane for Tactile Navigation Guidance" In: Proceedings of the California State University Northridge Center on Disabilities 25th Annual International Technology and Persons with Disabilities Conference (CSUN 2010), March 22-27, San Diego, CA, USA, 2010. [Online]. Available from: https://pdfs.semanticscholar.org/058a/fc0c1473984ddf75de2100ab108d94ace167.pdf 2018.01.01

[15] W.B. Albery, "Multisensory cueing for enhancing orientation information during flight. Aviation Space and Environmental Medicine, May 2007, 78(5s), B186-190.

[16] S.M. Ko, K. Lee, D. Kim, and Y.G. Ji, "Vibrotactile perception assessment for a haptic interface on an antigravity suit" Applied Ergonomics, Volume 58, pp. 198-207, January 2017.

[17] United Nations, Convention on the Rights of Persons with Disabilities. [Online]. Available from: http://www.un.org/disabilities/documents/convention/convoptprot-e.pdf 2018.01.30

Trusted Mobile Zone Solution Based on Virtualization Technology

GeonLyang Kim, JeongNyeo Kim
Information Security Research Division
Electronics and Telecommunications Research Institute
Daejeon, Republic of Korea
e-mail: glkim@etri.re.kr, jnkim@etri.re.kr

***Abstract*—We developed a Trusted Mobile Zone (TMZ) solution based on virtualization technology for smart mobile devices. This solution offers users a trusted execution area to preserve significant files, and execute security services in a secure manner. In addition, it is able to block attackers from leaking significant files. We simulated a Smishing attack to obtain significant data from a Secure Zone (SZ) of the TMZ solution, the results of which are described herein.**

Keywords-BYOD; Mobile Security; TEE; Virtualization.

I. Introduction

As the use of mobile devices rapidly increases, personal smart mobile devices are being used for business purposes. Solutions for blocking the outflow of enterprise files, such as Knox [1] and Cellrox [2], are urgently needed. We developed the Trusted Mobile Zone (TMZ) solution to offer better data leakage prevention services to users. Unlike Knox and Cellrox, the security functions of the TMZ solution operate on a secure OS different from a normal OS, and the proposed solution therefore has the advantage of being less vulnerable to malicious codes or attacks aiming at obtaining significant files by exploiting the vulnerabilities of a normal OS. The TMZ solution was designed with reference to the Global Platform's Trusted Execution Environment (TEE) system [3]. It offers a trusted execution area to preserve significant files and provide trusted services securely through secure components.

II. TMZ Solution Architecture

The TMZ solution supplies a higher level of security without paying additional costs through the addition of hardware [4]. The hypervisor as a virtualization technology has two types: a type 1 hypervisor as a native or bare-metal hypervisor, and a type 2 hypervisor as a hosted hypervisor [5]. A type 1 hypervisor offers a higher level of security than a type 2 hypervisor.

The TMZ solution can be built on a mobile device regardless of the hypervisor type applied. KNOX runs on Android OS, and provides kernel-level access control through SE Android. Most products including Horizon Mobile of VMWare offer the only separation of an Open OS and a Secure OS. However, the TMZ solution separates the General Zone (GZ) and SZ using a hypervisor. It also provides trusted security services for users through the use of security components including the SZ. The security components of the TMZ solution provide users with functions to store significant data, create signature data, deposit encryption and decryption keys, and preserve private keys for signature data, all in a secure manner. It also offers an encrypted communication channel for transmitting significant data securely between a GZ and an SZ. The architecture of the TMZ solution is shown in Figure 1.

The only GZ-Security API in a GZ is able to access an SZ through an encrypted communication channel. We defined the GZ-Security API of five groups and developed security applications that can offer trusted security services using an SZ through the GZ-Security API.

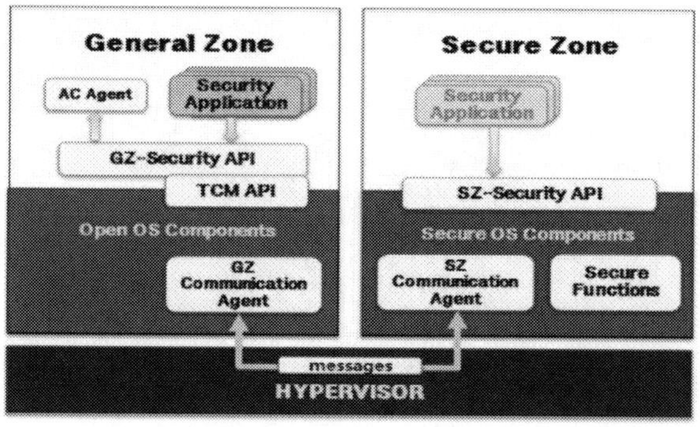

Figure 1. TMZ solution architecture

III. Data Leakage Prevention Services Using the TMZ Solution

We implemented data leakage prevention services, including a Trusted Certificate Store Service, Trusted Contact Service, Trusted Camera Service, and Trusted Gallery Service, using the TMZ solution. When hacking tools are used, general files in a GZ are spilled out, whereas significant files managed in an SZ are not spilled into a GZ or to the outside.

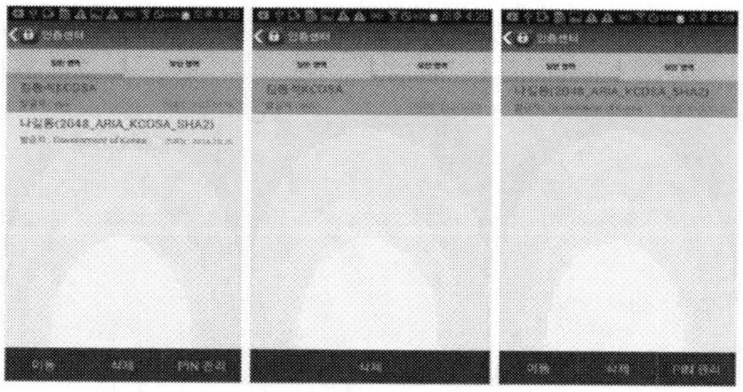

Figure 2. Screen shots of Trusted Certificate Service

Certificate files, including the private key file, are saved and managed in general storage that attackers are able to easily enter or release to the outside. Therefore, they are threatened by leaks and misuse by malicious users. If they are leaked to the outside, their owners can suffer damage through illegal authentication.

With a Trusted Certificate Service, the certificate files in a GZ are saved and managed in an SZ of the TMZ solution. This blocks the outflow of significant files for illegal authentication. The files are securely encrypted and managed in the SZ. Significant files, such as encryption key files, sensitive image files, and important contact files cannot be spilled out of the SZ into a GZ, and are secure.

IV. Smishing Attack Simulation on TMZ Solution

We proposed the TMZ solution for blocking the illegal outflow of significant files. The TMZ solution supplies a trusted execution area isolated from the GZ, where a large number of threats can occur and many vulnerabilities exist. The SZ operates on a different secure OS through Android OS of the NZ. This is more secure because the weaknesses of Android OS are not applicable to a secure OS. Therefore, the TMZ solution supplies trusted security services to users.

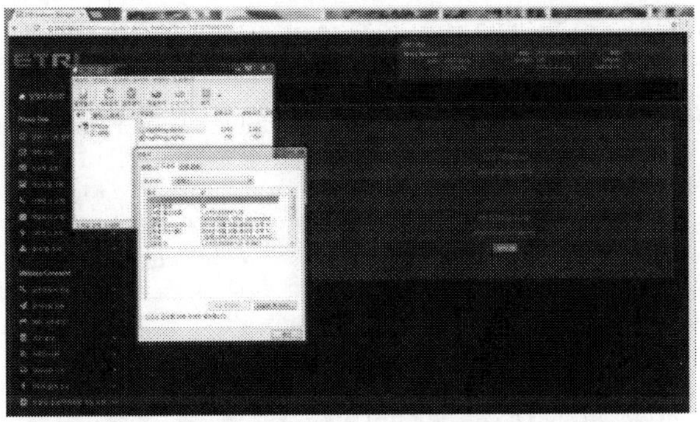

Figure 3. Files spilled out of GZ and into a hacking server

We simulated a Smishing attack to obtain significant data from an SZ of the TMZ solution. When a user applying the TMZ solution receives a Short Message Service (SMS) message and connects to a URL link in the message, a hacking application is installed and run.

After the hacking application is installed and executed through the message used in the Smishing attack, the general files in the GZ of the TMZ solution are transmitted to the hacking server. The user using the TMZ solution should manage their significant files in an SZ to block their outflow, including certificate files, contact files, and important image files.

Figure 3 shows files leaked from the hacking application of the GZ to the hacking server. The files transmitted from the TMZ solution to the hacking server through the hacking application are general files in the GZ of the TMZ solution. Figure 2 shows the certificate files in the GZ and SZ of the TMZ solution. We are able to know that the files spilled out from the TMZ solution and into the hacking server were the certificate files stored in the GZ of the TMZ solution.

V. Experiment Results

We calculated the time required to insert the certificate files securely from a GZ to an SZ. We built ETRI's VIMO type 2 hypervisor on Galaxy S3, and built μC/OS-II as a secure OS in the SZ for the TMZ solution. We calculated the required time 20 times in both the SZ and the GZ, the results of which are shown in Figure 4.

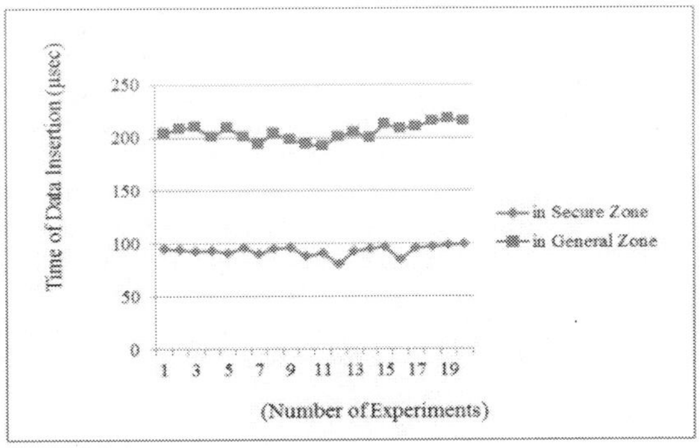

Figure 4. Performance measurement results

The calculated average value of insertion of certificate files in the GZ is 205 μsec, and in the SZ is 93 μsec.

VI. Conclusion

In this paper, we proposed a TMZ solution for blocking the illegal outflow of significant files. We simulated a Smishing attack to obtain significant files from the TMZ solution, and the files of SZ in the TMZ solution are not leaked. The TMZ solution can supply several security services by blocking the outflow of significant files in an SZ isolated from a GZ.

Acknowledgment

This work was supported by an Institute for Information & Communications Technology Promotion (IITP) grant funded by the Korea government (MSIT) [No. 2015-0-00508, Development of Operating System Security Core Technology for the Smart Lightweight IoT Devices].

References

[1] https://www.samsungknox.com/docs/SamsungKnoxSecuritySolution.pdf, Samsung Knox White Paper: Samsung KNOX Security Solution Version 2.2, May 2017.

[2] Cellrox Homepage, http://cellrox.com, March 2018.

[3] https://www.globalplatform.org/specificationsdevice.asp, "TEE System Architecture v1.1," Global Platform, January 2017.

[4] D. Jaramillo, B. Furht, and A. Agarwal, "Virtualization Techniques for Mobile Systems," Multimedia Systems and Applications, Springer International Publishing, 2014.

[5] G. J. Popek, R. P. Goldberg, "Formal Requirements for Virtualizable Third Generation Architectures," Communications of the ACM, 17(7):412-421, 1974.

Utility of a Mobile Route Planning App for People Aging with Disability

Jon A. Sanford, Sarah Melgen
Center for Assistive Technology and Environmental Access (CATEA)
Georgia Institute of Technology
Atlanta, GA
e-mails: jon.sanford@design.gatech.edu, sarah.melgen@design.gatech.edu

Subhrajit Guhathakurta, Ge Zhang
Center for Graphic Information Systems
Georgia Institute of Technology
Atlanta, GA
emails: subhro.guha@design.gatech.edu, gezhang@gmail.com

***Abstract* - Mobility is a key contributor to an individual's community living and participation. As a result, outdoor environmental barriers, such as uneven sidewalks and no curb cuts, play a crucial role in the development of disability and loss of independence among individuals aging with mobility and vision limitations. To compensate, people with disabilities typically plan routes before going out. However, they often lack the appropriate street-level information about the environment to plan routes that meet their abilities and needs for safety and accessibility (e.g., the location of curb cuts and crosswalks). As a result, the real impediment to outdoor mobility is not the actual barriers, but the lack of information about those barriers for route planning. To provide the street-level information about barriers that would maximize the independent living and community participation of people with mobility disabilities, the project team developed a working prototype of the Application for Locational Intelligence and Geospatial Navigation (ALIGN) based on static graphical information systems (GIS) data (e.g., physical infrastructure, slope, crime rates and land uses). This study details the utility testing of the application with individuals aging with mobility and vision limitations by using direct observation, think-aloud and open-ended questionnaires. Findings indicate that participants found the application to be potentially useful, especially in unfamiliar locations. However, testing also indicated a number of refinements, including multimodal input and outputs that would enhance the utility of the initial prototype. Additional design criteria will inform the next prototype, including use of consistent audio/visual feedback, and simpler directions. These criteria will be applied to create a more usable application for the target population.**

Keywords-mobile wayfinding; assistive technology; aging in place.

I. INTRODUCTION

From the need for basic exercise, to more complex participatory behaviors, such as grocery shopping, going to the doctor and visiting friends, mobility is a key contributor to an individual's community living and participation. For older adults and individuals with disabilities, outdoor mobility is especially important to successfully to maintain independence, physical and mental health, and quality of life [1][2]. Not surprisingly, outdoor environmental barriers, such as uneven sidewalks and no curb cuts, play a crucial role in the development of mobility disability among individuals with a range of functional limitations [3]. Whereas removing physical barriers in the U.S. has been ongoing for more than a quarter century since the passage of the Americans with Disabilities Act in 1990, it is an expensive and long-term process that will likely continue for many years to come.

To compensate for environmental barriers, people with disabilities typically plan routes before going out [4]. Community activities are organized in advance to formulate strategies that address, for example, the inaccessibility of routes, distances travelled and terrain. However, the appropriate street-level information about the environmental attributes (e.g., the location of curb cuts and crosswalks) that are needed to plan routes that meet an individual's own abilities and needs is often lacking. As a result, the real barrier to outdoor mobility may not be the actual environment itself, but the lack of information that would empower individuals with mobility impairments to plan safe, accessible and situationally-appropriate routes based on their own abilities, needs and preferences.

Whereas creating totally barrier-free environments is an ideal goal, providing environmental information for individualized route planning is a comparatively inexpensive and short-term process that could immediately impact community mobility for seniors with a mobility disability. To provide the type of street-level information about barriers that would maximize the community mobility for these individuals, the project team developed a working prototype of the *Application for Locational Intelligence and Geospatial Navigation* (ALIGN) based on static graphical information systems (GIS) data (e.g., physical infrastructure, slope, crime rates and land uses). This paper reports on the usefulness of the application in providing mobility assistance to people aging with vision and ambulatory limitations.

The second section of this paper details the current practices of and barriers to pedestrian mobility, as well as the available resources to help with travel route decision-making. Section 3 describes the prototype design, and the research methods used to test the application's utility. The results outlined in Section 4 give insight to the errors made in observation of route navigation, in addition to the post-trial questionnaire responses. Finally, Section 5 discusses the implications of these results and recommendations for the application's next iteration.

II. Background

Community mobility is both a means and an end. As a means, it is a way to get from one place to another. As an end, it is an activity that is the most commonly reported form of physical activity that has demonstrated a variety of health benefits [5]-[7].

Despite the positive impact of environmental facilitators, such as curb cuts, tactile warnings and audible pedestrian signals, people with disabilities routinely encounter difficulties while either "walking" or "wheeling" in their communities, even on routes that are "accessible" under the 2010 Americans with Disabilities Act Standards for Accessible Design [8]. Barriers not covered in the standards (e.g., long distances, steep slopes, high curbs, wide streets and short traffic lights), can deter traveling in the community, thus compromising health, independence and overall quality of life.

Numerous studies have linked restricted community mobility among people with disabilities to the wide range of barriers and hazards, many that compromise safety (e.g., crossing a busy intersection) and increase fatigue due to maneuvering around obstacles (e.g., a pole in the middle of a sidewalk). Specific barriers identified in the literature include: curbs, lack of curb ramps, sidewalk availability, poor drainage, narrow pathways; hilly or steep topography; ramp availability, presence of crosswalks, availability of resting places and shelters, lack of accessible parking, presence of water fountains, bathrooms, and rest areas; unsafe neighborhoods, and inclement weather [2][3][9]-[13].

Individuals with disabilities generally use familiar outdoor routes that fit their functional abilities and assistive technologies. However, for those who are experiencing the additive effects of age-related declines, environmental barriers continually pose new sets of challenges that can further limit mobility even on long-used routes [14][15] leading to mobility restricted participation in multiple activities outside the home [16]. In fact, limitations in walking for exercise is secondary to restricted access to a variety of community destinations, including grocery stores, senior centers, drug stores and places of worship [17]. Most importantly, these restrictions not only lead to further decline in function, but also have broader implications for nutrition, medical care, and other community services that are crucial to independence, social connectedness, health and well-being of seniors with disabilities.

To aid pedestrian route planning, many navigation apps, such as *Google Maps, Co-Pilot, Mapquest and Waze*, have walking functions that provide voice-guided turn-by-turn directions similar to their driving functions. In addition, there are a growing number of mobile applications that are intended to promote walking by assessing the pedestrian friendliness of an area and translating this information into a walking score. Most (e.g., *Walkscore.com, Walkonomics.com* and *Walkshed.org)* provide information about environmental factors, such as access to amenities, residential density, street connectivity, land use diversity, traffic safety and crime safety that influence walking behavior and route decision-making [18][19]. Whereas many of the attributes included in these applications are relevant to people with mobility disabilities, few, if any, of the applications include the environmental characteristics that would address the specific needs of people with aging with mobility disability.

Similarly, there are a growing number of mobility applications for individuals with disabilities. Among these, *Rollstuhlrouting* (wheelchair routing) is the only online application that includes environmental factors to inform route planning for wheelchair users. However, this portal uses only 3 infrastructure parameters: slope (4% – 12% in 2% increments and any slope), surface material (4 types) and curb heights (3cm – 11cm in 2cm increments and any height) that are deemed necessary for wheelchair accessible routes. Two newer applications, *IBM Accessible Way* and *PathVu*, use crowd-sourcing approaches to gather street-level accessibility information, such as mobility barriers, poor sidewalk conditions and absence of lighting, tactile paving, curb ramps, and crosswalks. However, these applications are not only dependent on volunteer data, which has implications for the reliability of the data, but are also focused solely on wheelchair accessibility, which limits their generalizability to people aging with various disabilities. Environmental features that are perceived as safe and accessible by one individual may be viewed very differently by individuals with different functional abilities, preferences, motivations, support systems and tolerance for risk.

Most importantly, decision-making about travel routes tends to be situational and idiosyncratic, unique to individuals and to a particular point in time, and often dependent upon an individual's ability to make an accurate assessment of the accessibility, safety and desirability of a route. To do so, the main challenge is to obtain environmental information that individuals do not have in order to identify and potentially avoid routes that include environmental barriers, as well as to factor in other situational variables, such as time, distance and safety. Without such information, the most expedient solution is to avoid traveling in the community altogether, which partly explains reduced levels of activity and exercise among seniors and people with disabilities.

To overcome limitations in the existing walkability and accessibility applications, the project team developed ALIGN, a mobile route planning application that not only considers the salient physical environmental factors that impact accessibility and safe mobility, but also an individual's personal and social motivations and preferences that influence route planning. Most importantly, based on an array of essential and secondary user preferences, ALIGN not only prioritizes alternative routes, but also identifies the location of potential barriers where routes do not meet user requirements. This paper reports on the initial prototype testing to evaluate its usefulness by people aging with disability prior to full-scale deployment and testing.

III. Methods

A. Research Design

The study used a mixed methods approach in an outdoor setting to determine the usefulness of the application. This included direct observation of the application in use, thinking out loud to record participant feedback during app use and post-test questionnaire to obtain user feedback about the application. Direct observation of participant behavior while completing a series of routine tasks (e.g., select parameters, input a destination, choose a route, follow the route) enabled the study team to record objective data about errors made including difficulty finding the correct buttons and avoidance of the 'problem area' icons in the laboratory usability study, veering off course outdoors, backtracking, pausing/confusion, and wrong turns on the outdoor route. Thinking out loud provided opportunities to obtain subjective participant experience about underlying problems that were not evident or had to be inferred from direct observation (e.g., confusion, how often they would like audio/visual feedback). Similarly, post-test questionnaires, provided an opportunity for participant feedback through a series of questions with Likert scale levels of agreement (where 1=strongly disagree to 5=strong agree) and open-ended questions about the usability of specific features of the application, as well as their overall impression of the application. Questions were used to gauge how participants felt about the application's potential, and where there were subjective errors and room for improvement.

B. Prototype Test Application (ALIGN 1.0)

ALIGN is built on: 1) environmental factors based on existing walkability and accessibility literature that are applicable to route planning decisions by individuals with mobility disabilities; 2) a database structure and data acquisition processes to import the validated factors; 3) a weighting system applied to each factor based on an Analytical Hierarchy Process (AHP) that generates mobility scores for route segments; 4) implementation of a routing algorithm; and 5) a simple and intuitive user interface based on universal design principles.

The prototype application (Fig. 1) enables users to select from a number of mobility factors, including accessibility factors (e.g., slope, presence of curb ramps) and other static infrastructure factors (e.g., land uses, vegetation, street connectivity) based on their own needs and desires. A variety of readily available GIS sources were used to automatically capture much of the environmental data. As a result, ALIGN databases and algorithms are updated at the same time as the original sources. We used the street network data from 2007 Georgia Dept. of Transportation and the Atlanta Regional Commission street file. Block boundary data were obtained from 2010 U.S. Census Bureau TIGER/Line shape files. A measure of intersection density was calculated using the ArcGIS network analysis tool based on the street network data. The variables in the residential density group were calculated using the ArcGIS operator tool based on the 2010 U.S. census block data. Similarly, the variables in the business density, land use mix diversity and land use mix accessibility categories were calculated using the ArcGIS operator tool, zonal analysis tool and Euclidean distance tool, based on the 2012 reference USA business database. Crime data were obtained from the Atlanta Police. Slope was calculated using the ArcGIS 3D analysis tool, based on the 1999 digital elevation model data (30 meters pixel resolution) provided by the U.S. Geological Survey (USGS). ERDAS 9.3 Indices tool was used to quantify vegetation coverage based on the 2011 Landsat image data provided by the USGS. Traffic volume was obtained from the 2009 average annual daily traffic data provided by the GA Department of Transportation (GDOT). Public transit data were collected from the 2010 GA Regional Transportation Authority. Finally, sidewalk data were obtained from the GDOT.

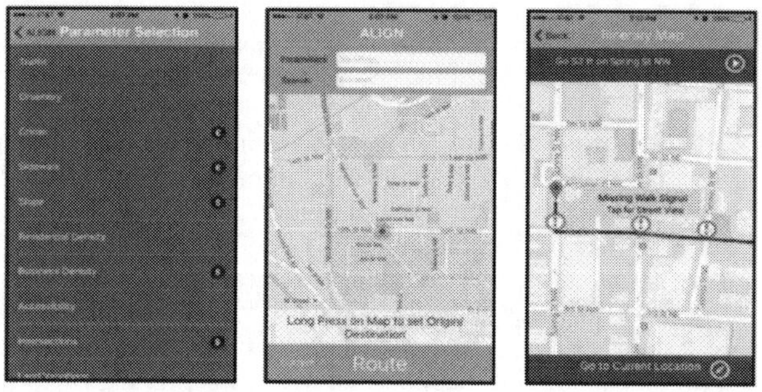

Figure 1. Prototype screenshots of the parameter selection page, the map landing page, and a sample route showing parameter errors

A number of key environmental factors were not available in any systematic GIS dataset, including the presence of curb cuts, crosswalks, traffic signals and intersection type. To capture these types of data, a data collection protocol was developed to capture and record environmental features of interest directly from *Google Streetview*.

Ideally, the ALIGN mobile application would be able to create routes that cater to all possible combinations of essential environmental factors (referred to henceforth as parameters). However, in most cases, it is unrealistic that any nearby route would be able to fit all criteria. Thus, a maximum of five essential parameters (and unlimited secondary parameters) can be selected in order to create a useful tool that allows users to be able to choose the parameters that are essential for their walking routes, for their flexibility, as well as their safety.

C. Test Environment

Three routes were laid out at the eastern edge of Georgia Tech's campus and extending into the adjacent neighboring community of Midtown, Atlanta. All three routes (Fig. 2) had the same starting point. However, each route had a different destination and the numbers and types of potential mobility barriers. The destinations varied in length and complexity. The simplest (to Starbucks 1 on the map) was one block and included crossing a street with a missing walk signal. The second route was two blocks (to Starbucks 2) without any potential mobility barriers. The third route was three blocks (to the Center for the Visually Impaired) and included an intersection with no crosswalk or traffic signal.

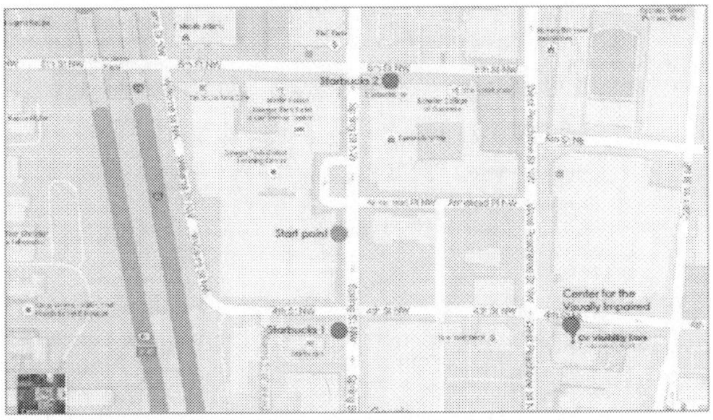

Figure 2. Map of observation routes

D. Procedures

After consenting to participate in a test protocol approved by the Georgia Tech Institutional Review Board, participants were given the ALIGN application on a mobile device. All participants were given the same minimal description of how to use the application so as not to bias its use. Participants were instructed to complete two of three test routes, selected at random. A researcher walking along with the participant recorded errors made including: veering off course, backtracking, pause/confusion, and wrong turns. Each error was noted as 'self-corrected' by the participant or 'team-corrected' by the researcher. It was also noted where participants asked for help and when it was provided. Following each trial, participants were asked to provide their level of agreement (on a 1-5 Likert scale where 1= strongly disagree to 5 = strongly agree) with items regarding the usefulness of the app.

IV. Results

A. Sample

Thirteen (13) individuals 50+ years of age with a self-reported ambulatory and/or vision limitation for at least 5 years that affected their mobility in outdoor environments were recruited for the study. Participants were recruited from local retirement communities, as well as three GA Tech participant registries: HomeLab, a registry of over 500 seniors who have agreed to participate in in-home and community studies; the CATEA Consumer Network, a registry of adults with disabilities; and the TechSAge Registry, a registry of older adults with disabilities.

Of the 13 participants included, three were men and ten were women. Seven participants had some degree of vision loss and eight had some degree of mobility impairment with two participants reporting having both vision and mobility limitations. Subjects ranged in age from 50 to 76 years of age, with a mean age of 63.8 years. Education levels varied amongst the participants – two had vocational training, four had some college or associate's degree, two had received bachelor's degrees, one had a master's degree, and two participants had received PhDs.

B. Observation Data

Table I shows the observed and stated errors during the outdoor observation route. Some participants made repeated errors, which are noted accordingly in the overall number of instances (i.e., 10 participants paused on their route 17 times total on their collective routes). The results are spread more or less evenly across demographics, with the exception of the two low vision participants who veered off-course.
Of note, 9 participants missed or did not recognize their destination, which can be attributed to the lack of a visual or audio notification that they had arrived at their destination. Similarly, 9 participants who had warnings that the route had missing walk signals did not see or hear the warning.

Finally, half (n=5) of the participants paused at intersections to look at the application. Nonetheless, of the 17 times the 10 participants paused or were confused, all were self-corrected. In contrast, there were only 2 instances of wrong turns and 2 instances of veering off course and 3 of the 4 were self corrected.

TABLE I. Observed errors on outdoor route

	Pause/Confusion		**Wrong turn**		**Veering off-course**		**Help**		
	Self - corrected	*Team - corrected*	*Self - corrected*	*Team - corrected*	*Self - corrected*	*Team - corrected*	*Asked*	*Provided*	*Asked and provided*
Overall # of instances	17	0	1	1	2	0	2	2	8
Overall # of participants	10	0	1	1	2	0	2	2	5
Participants w/ low vision	6	0	0	1	2	0	1	2	3
Participants w/ low mobility	4	0	1	0	0	0	1	0	2
Participants< 65 years	5	0	1	0	1	0	2	2	2
Participants≥ 65 years	5	0	0	1	1	0	0	0	3

C. Post-Trial Questionnaire

Most notably, participants strongly agreed (mean = 4.58) that the mobility factors met their needs for route planning. In fact, when queried about the need for additional factors 11 of 13 participants did not see room for any additional parameters, while two suggested adding factors that are not necessary for safe mobility (i.e., accessibility of doors in buildings and nearby places to eat).

In response to the statement that the app would be helpful for navigating as a pedestrian, the mean response of 3.38, or slightly above neutral. In contrast, the mean response to the statement that it would be easier to navigate as a pedestrian with the application than without it was 4.0 or agree. However, when asked if they would use the app, six of the participants responded that they would use it, if it worked perfectly. In addition, 4 participants stated that the app would be easier to use once they were able to familiarize themselves with it.

Finally, when asked if there were any unexpected barriers in using the application, 10 participants provided recommendations for refinement, including: the ability to input location names (i.e., Publix) instead of only addresses; providing notification upon arrival at a destination and more feedback from the application as a whole; providing cardinal directions; user-friendly terminology; and reducing the learning curve when first using the app.

V. Conclusion and Future Work

Participants reported that, overall, the application was more beneficial than not. Moreover, it is likely to be used, if it is working properly and more user friendly. However, this will require refinements before the application is ready for prime time. Clearly, consistent participant feedback about the lack of auditory input and output, as well as noticeable route errors, such as missing the destination, suggest that there is need for consistent feedback to the user. While the prototype was tested prior to the implementation of these interfaces, the planned addition of voice control (e.g., voice command option on the map screen) and audio, visual and tactile feedback in v. 1.1 (e.g., audio feedback at turns and barriers) should increase usefulness and usability of the application. In addition, utility will be enhanced in v.1.1 by the inclusion of other participant recommendations including a tutorial when first opening the app, inputting location names, use of more user friendly terminology and option for cardinal directions.

Acknowledgements

This work was supported by the National Institute on Disability, Independent Living, and Rehabilitation Research (NIDILRR) under the Rehabilitation Engineering Research Center (RERC) TechSAge [grant number *90RE5016-01-00*].

References

[1] R. Hjorthol, "Transport resources, mobility and unmet transport needs in old age." Ageing and Society, vol. 33, no. 7, pp. 1190-1211, 2013.

[2] C. Kochtitzky, A.L. Freeland, and I. H. Yen, "Ensuring Mobility-Supporting Environments for an Aging Population: Critical Actors and Collaborations," Journal of Aging Research doi:10.4061/2011/138931, vol. 2011(2011), 10 pgs, 2011.

[3] J. J. Keysor, A.M Jette, M.P La Valley, C. E. Lewis, J. C. Tomer, and M.C. Nevitt, "Community environmental factors are associated with disability in older adults with functional limitations: the MOST study," The Journal of Gerontology. Series A, Biological Sciences and Medical Sciences, vol. 65, pp. 393-399, 2010.

[4] C. Kirchner, E. G. Gerber, and B. C. Smith, "Designed to deter: Community barriers to physical activity for people with visual or motor impairments," American Journal of Preventive Medicine, vol. 34, no. 4, pp. 349-352, 2008.

[5] L. D. Frank and P. O. Engelke, "The built environment and human activity patterns: Exploring the impacts of urban form on public health." J Plan Lit vol. 16, no. 2, pp. 202-218, 2001.

[6] B. E. Saelens, J. F. Sallis, and L. D. Frank, "Environmental correlates of walking and cycling: Findings from the transportation, urban design, and planning literatures." Ann Behav Med vol. 25, no. 2, pp. 80-91. 2003.

[7] V. Lathey, S. Guhathakurta, and R. M. Aggarwal, "The Impact of Subregional Variations in Urban Sprawl on the Prevalence of Obesity and Related Morbidity." J Plan Educ Res vol. 29, no. 2, pp. 127-141, 2009.

[8] Department of Justice. "2010 ADA Standards for Accessible Design," Retrieved December 2017 from http://www.asa.gov/regs2010/2010ADAStandards/2010ADAstandards.htm, 2010.

[9] H. Becker and A. Stuifbergen, "Barriers to health promotion experienced by people with multiple sclerosis and polio." Fam & Community Health, vol. 27, pp. 75-85, 2004.

[10] Chaudhury, A. Mahmood, Y. L. Michael, M. Campo, and K. Hay, "The influence of neighborhood residential density, physical and social environments.on older adults' physical activity: an exploratory study in two metropolitan areas." Journal of Aging Studies, vol. 26, pp. 35–43, 2012.

[11] N. Humpel, N. Owen, and E. Leslie, "Environmental factors associated with adults' participation in physical activity: A review," American Journal of Preventive Medicine, vol. 22, no. 3, pp. 188-199, 2002.

[12] A. R. Meyers, J. J. Anderson, D. R. Miller, K. Shipp, and H. Hoenig, "Barriers, facilitators, and access for wheelchair users: sbstantive and methodologic lessons from a pilot study of environmental effects." *Social Science & Medicine*, vol. *55*, no. 8, pp. 1435-1446, 2002.

[13] J. H. Rimmer, B. Riley, E. Wang, A. Rauworth, J. Jurkowski, "Physical activity participation among persons with disabilities: barriers and facilitators." Am J Prev Med, vol. 26, pp. 419-425, 2004.

[14] M. Rantakokko, S. Iwarsson, M. Mänty, R. Leinonen, and T. Rantanen, "Perceived barriers in the outdoor environment and development of walking difficulties in older people." Age and Ageing, vol. 41, no. 1, pp. 118-121, 2012.

[15] A. L. Rosso, A. H. Auchincloss, and Y. L. Michael, "The Urban Built Environment and Mobility in Older Adults: A Comprehensive Review." Journal of Aging Research, Article ID 816106, 10 pages doi:10.4061/2011/816106, 2011.

[16] H. Hoenig, L. R. Landerman, K. M. Shipp, and L. George, "Activity restriction among wheelchair users." Journal of the

American Geriatrics Society, vol. 51, no. 9, pp. 1244-1251, 2003.

[17] D. E. Rosenberg, D. L. Huang, S. D. Simonovch, and B. Belza, "Outdoor built environment barriers and facilitators to activity among midlife and older adults with mobility disabilities," The Gerontologist, vol. 53, no. 2, pp. 268-279, 2013.

[18] E. Leslie et al., "Residents' perceptions of walkability attributes in objectively different neighbourhoods: a pilot study," Health and Place vol. 11, pp. 227-236, 2007.

[19] E. Cerin, B. E. Saelens, J. F. Sallis, and L. D. Frank, "Neighborhood environment walkability scale: Validity and development of a short form." Med Sci Sport Exer vol. 38, no. 9, pp. 1682-1691, 2006.

A Qualitative Approach to Understanding User Needs for Aging with Disability

Elena T. Remillard &
Tracy L. Mitzner
Center for Assistive Technology
and Environmental Access
Georgia Institute of Technology
Atlanta, GA, USA
email: tracy@gatech.edu
elena.remillard@design.gatech.edu

Jenny L. Singleton
School of Psychology
Gerogia Institute of Technology,
Atlanta, GA, USA
email: jenny.singleton@gatech.edu

Wendy A. Rogers
College of Applied Health Sciences
University of Illinois
Urbana-Champaign, IL, USA
email: wendyr@illinois.edu

Abstract— **There is a growing population of adults with long-term sensory and mobility impairments who are aging into older adulthood. Little is known about the everyday challenges and accessibility issues experienced by these individuals as they age and acquire age-related declines in addition to a pre-existing impairment. The present paper provides an overview of a large-scale interview study, currently in progress, exploring user needs of older adults with long-term vision, hearing, and mobility impairments. The structured interview is designed to elicit detailed information on task performance challenges across a wide range of daily activities, as well as strategies to manage those challenges. In this paper we provide case-study examples from each of the three impairment groups to convey the potential depth and breadth of insights about user needs among individuals aging with impairments that can be realized through this novel qualitative approach.**

Keywords-aging; disability; technology; impairment; Deaf/hard of hearing; vision impairment; mobility impairment.

I. INTRODUCTION

Worldwide, advances in healthcare, rehabilitation, and technology are enabling individuals with impairments to live longer lives than ever before. In the U.S., nearly 40% of older adults (over age 65) reported having one or more disabilities, including vision (19% of those with disabilities), hearing (40%), and ambulatory (67%) impairments [1]. Despite the prevalence of older adults with sensory and mobility impairments, very little is known about the segment of this population who acquired their impairments in early or mid-life, said to be "aging with disability" [2][3]. An estimated 12 – 15 million adults in the U.S are aging with impairments that began prior to age 40 [4]. For these individuals, the addition of normative age-related changes, such as declines in vision, cognition, and motor functioning, can create new barriers in carrying out everyday activities and increase the likelihood of disability.

Technology holds great potential to support older adults with long-term impairments in maintaining daily activities and living as independently as possible [5]. To effectively design technologies that meet the needs of these individuals, it is necessary to understand more about the experiences of people aging with impairment. How do their support needs change across the lifespan? Are the same assistive technologies that someone used as a child, or as younger adult, still effective for them as an older adult? How do new impairments and chronic conditions impact routines for everyday activities? To begin answering these questions, researchers must engage the individuals who are experiencing aging with impairment first-hand.

Currently in progress, the Aging Concerns, Challenges, and Everyday Solution Strategies (ACCESS) study is a large-scale, mixed method study investigating user needs of individuals aging with impairment. This project is part of the Technologies to Support Successful Aging with Disability Center (TechSAge). The goal of the ACCESS study is to understand the nature and distribution of task performance problems with everyday activities for older adults with long-term vision, hearing, or mobility impairment. In addition to activity challenges, the study explores the various strategies individuals in these three distinct populations employ to manage them. The ACCESS study utilizes both quantitative (questionnaires) and qualitative (structured interview) methods to assess perceptions of task difficulty and the nature of participants' challenges and solutions.

The current paper provides a brief overview of the interview component of the study and presents case study examples that convey the potential value of this novel approach in understanding user needs for this understudied population. In section 2, the study methods are described with regard to participant characteristics, materials (interview guide and questionnaires), procedures, accommodations for participants with sensory impairments, and analysis. Section 3 is comprised of case study examples from a participant in each of the three target populations (n=3). This section includes a table with descriptive characteristics about the participant sample as well as examples of challenges mentioned in the interview. Finally, Section 4 features a discussion of the emerging findings from the analysis of case study examples and implications for the qualitative component of the broader study in progress.

II. METHOD

A. *Participants*

The goal of the ACCESS study is to enroll 60 participants in each of the three target populations (vision, hearing, mobility; total n = 180). To be eligible for this study, participants must be between the ages of 60 and 79 and have a vision, hearing, or mobility impairment that began prior to age 50. There are additional inclusion criteria specific to each impairment group. Vision participants must self-identify as Blind or Low Vision, operationally defined as "unable to see" or "having serious difficulty seeing even when wearing glasses or contact lenses." Participants in the Hearing impairment group must self-identify as Deaf or hard of hearing and use American Sign Language (ASL) as their primary language for communication. Mobility participants must self-identify as having a mobility impairment and either use a mobility aid or have serious difficulty walking or climbing stairs. All participants must live in the Unites States and be able to complete the interview in English or ASL.

Participants to date were primarily recruited through outreach to local and national disability resource organizations and conferences as well as from the Georgia Institute of Technology Human Factors and Aging Participant Registry and the University of Illinois Disability Resources and Education Services Research Registry. Participants receive $30 USD compensation for completing the questionnaires (1 hour) and interview (1-1.5 hours).

B. Materials

1) Interview guide: A structured interview guide was developed to elicit participants' challenges with everyday activities as well as the strategies they employ to overcome those challenges. The scope of activities covered in the interview guide was selected based on findings from an earlier study wherein subject matter experts with personal and/or professional experiences with older adults with sensory and mobility impairments (e.g., caregivers, medical professionals) gave their perspectives on the challenges experienced by these populations [6].

For each activity category, there is a rating activity followed by open-ended interview questions. The purpose of the rating activity is to identify which specific types of activities are the most difficult for participants to do. Participants rate topics within the activity category based on how difficult it is for them to do using a 3-point scale (1 = not at all difficult, 2 = a little difficult, 3 = very difficult, or N/A = not applicable). The interviewer uses a worksheet to document the difficulty ratings for each topic. Participants are instructed to give ratings based on the way they currently do the activity now, including any help or support they receive. Once all ratings have been provided, the interviewer reviews the worksheet to identify the topic with the highest difficulty rating which will be the subject of follow-up, open-ended questions. Following the rating activity, there are open-ended questions that focus on overall activity category, and how activities may have changed as they have gotten older. These questions were designed to capture how participants are adapting their activity routines and managing challenges in relation to the Selection, Optimization, and Compensation (SOC) framework. Stemming for the aging literature, the SOC framework is used to describe how individuals adapt to developmental challenges across the life span via the processes of selection, optimization, and compensation [7]. Interview questions ask participants how they are handling their challenge in distinct ways by probing for different types of solutions they might be employing, such as using a technology or getting help from someone.

2) Questionnaires: The current paper focuses on the qualitative component of the study. However, participants also complete self-report questionnaires to assess demographic and individual charactistics (e.g., functional abilities, information about the nature and degree of participants' impairment).

C. Procedures

Eligible participants are scheduled for an interview appointment, which takes approximately 1-1.5 hours to complete. Interviews and are either conducted in-person or remotely via telephone or Video Phone, which is a common technology in most households with a Deaf resident. Participants located in Metro Atlanta GA or Champaign-Urbana IL have the option to complete the interview with a researcher or in-person.

Once the study is complete, audio recordings of the interview are transcribed into text files. For ASL video interviews, screen recording software is used to record the entire interview, onto which voice-over translation for both the interviewer and participant is later recorded. To ensure accuracy, ASL-to-English translations of completed interviews are conducted by hearing native ASL signers who are highly familiar with the project and the questions being asked. The voice-over English translations are then transcribed into text.

D. Accomodations

The study was designed with flexible administration options to accommodate participants with sensory impairments. In addition to the standard paper consent form, participants were provided with an audio recording of the content. Recognizing that some Deaf participants may have challenges reading English, the research team developed a summary of the consent form in ASL. Interviews with Deaf older adult participants are being conducted in ASL by interviewers who are also Deaf to ensure authenticity and cultural/linguistic appropriateness. One of the project investigators, who is fluent in ASL, worked with a native-signing sign language interpreter to develop a parallel ASL translation of the ACCESS Interview script. The Deaf interviewers were trained on all study procedures and completed necessary human subjects research certifications.

E. Analysis

As data collection continues, researchers are beginning to review interview transcripts and develop the coding scheme for qualitative analysis. The present paper presents examples of activity challenges as three case studies, one from each of the three impairment groups. Descriptive information regarding participant characteristics were compiled from responses to questionnaires.

III. Case Study Examples

The current paper presents initial insights from a participant in each of the three impairment groups (n = 3). Table 1 features descriptive characteristics about the participant sample as well as examples of challenges mentioned in the interview. For the purpose of this paper, the three participants are identified as V1, D1, & M1, with the letter signifying their respective impairment group (vision, hearing, and mobility). Participants represent distinct impairment characteristics with regard to type, onset age, underlying cause, nature (limitations/abilities), and use of supportive aids. Each participant reported having at least two chronic conditions, such as arthritis and diabetes.

Interviews with participants revealed a wide range of challenges across the different domains of activities, as depicted in Table 1. Quotation marks indicate a verbatim quote from the participant, whereas examples without quotations indicates that the researcher paraphrased the participant's comments. The topic that participants rated as the most difficult in each category is listed in parentheses alongside examples. Participants mentioned at least one challenge for each of the six categories, with the exception of Shopping and Finances category for which V1 did not report any challenges. In many cases, the topic participants identified as the most difficult in each category was different than that of their counterparts.

Most of the activity challenges mentioned were unique to each impairment group. In one instance, two participants, V1 and D1, shared the same most difficult topic (working, volunteering or other civic activities), but described distinct challenges relating to fatigue and communication barriers respectively. There were some activity challenges, however, that were shared among participants. For example, D1 and V1 both described challenges keeping track of medications due to forgetfulness. Similarly, D1 and M1 discussed changes in their physical abilities that have made housekeeping tasks more difficult overtime.

Participants generally attributed task performance problems to their primary impairment. For example, M1 discussed the extensive planning she has to do to ensure that group activities in the community are wheelchair accessible. One interesting finding is that each participant discussed a challenge that they did not attribute to their primary impairment, but rather to other conditions or aging. For example, V1 expressed that his challenge with grooming tasks, such as shaving and brushing his teeth, was remembering to do them; he attributed these memory issues to a recent brain tumor. Similarly, D1 discussed that she periodically gets vertigo and loses her balance, which can make it hard to move around at home.

All participants described needs that could potentially be addressed through technology innovations. Having multiple co-morbid conditions, V1 has a complicated medication regimen and could benefit from some kind of reminder system to help him take his medications as prescribed. D1 highlighted connectivity issues with Video Relay Interpreting (VRI) which could be improved in future development and refinement of the system. M1's trouble identifying whether or not a building is wheelchair accessible might be addressed through a website or mobile application that utilizes crowdsourced information on the presence or absence of accessible features within community venues. Regardless of what potential technology solutions might be appropriate, and whether such a solution currently exists, the interviews honed in on participants' user needs that are not currently being met.

IV. Discussion

Older adults with long-term sensory and mobility impairments are likely to experience challenges beyond those that accompany the normative aging process. There is a need for in-depth research that explores not only the activity challenges experienced by this population, but also the specific components of the task that create problems and could ultimately result in disability [8]. The ACCESS study is the first large-scale interview study exploring user needs among older adults with long-term vision, hearing, and mobility impairments. The interview was strategically designed to explore difficulty across a broad range of activities, while also probing for each participant's insights on activities that are particularly challenging for them. By incorporating a number of accommodations, including the training of Deaf interviewers to conduct interviews with Deaf older adult participants, the ACCESS study serves as a novel method to capture the perspectives of older adults with sensory and mobility impairments.

These case study examples (n = 3) convey the potential depth and breadth of insights on technology user needs of older adults with long-term sensory and mobility impairments that can be realized through this study. Interviews suggest that challenges experienced by these individuals are complex, and are subject to a variety of factors related to the person (e.g., capabilities and limitations, financial resources, support) and their environment (e.g., housing, community infrastructure, transportation). Moreover, it is clear that age-related declines and other co-morbid conditions are contributing to activity challenges among this population. This finding leads to the hypothesis that older adults with long-term impairments are not only likely to experience more challenges than non-impaired older adults, but also more than younger cohorts of people with the same types of impairments. The complexity of challenges revealed among just 3 individuals confirms the need to extend this research with a larger, more diverse group of individuals. Researchers continue data collection and analysis for the ACCESS study with the goal of developing a taxonomy of everyday support needs for individuals aging with impairment. Detailed user needs insights can ultimately guide the development of supportive and accessible technology solutions for individuals with impairments across the lifespan.

TABLE I. PARTICIPANT CHARACTERISTICS AND EXAMPLES OF ACTIVITY CHALLENGES MENTIONED IN THE INTERVIEW

	Vision - V1	**Deaf - D1**	**Mobility - M1**
Participant characteristics	Gender: male Age: 60 Age of impairment onset: birth Cause of impairment: Right eye not fully developed at birth Nature of impairment: No vision in right eye; able to read large print with left eye Use of visual supportive aids: Reading magnifier, scanners, optical character recognition (OCR) Chronic conditions: Arthritis, cancer, cardiac arrhythmia, depression, heart failure, hypertension, high cholesterol, overweight	Gender: female Age: 69 Age of impairment onset: 1 Cause of impairment: unknown Nature of impairment: impairment in both ears; even with use of hearing aid, cannot hear well enough to have a spoken conversation Use of hearing supportive aids: hearing aid, interpreter services, TTY, video phone Chronic conditions: High cholesterol, overweight	Gender: female Age: 70 Age of impairment onset: 6 Cause of impairment: multiple sclerosis and post-polio syndrome Nature of impairment: able to walk short distances with cane Use of supportive mobility aids: cane, manual wheelchair, scooter, knee brace, orthotic device Chronic conditions: asthma, arthritis, diabetes, hypertension, high cholesterol, overweight
Categories	**Examples of challenges from interview**		
Activities Outside the Home	It is challenging for him to participate with without getting short of breath or dizzy. (Working, volunteering or participating in other civic activities)	"If it is a group of all deaf people, it is fine. If there was some kind of activity with hearing people, then that would be difficult...I have to write with them and I hope they are patient writing with me." (Working volunteering or participating in other civic activities)	"I have to do a lot of pre-planning. I contact whoever is in charge to find out where it is, and if that place is upstairs, that is has an elevator. If getting there is a problem, I might have to use my wheelchair instead of my scooter, and then I have to find somebody to push it." (Doing things with a group or organization)
Things You Do Around the Home	He relies on his high-powered magnifier and sense of touch for fixing things around the home. It is hard because he can't see where a leak is coming from or what type of screw is needed. (Repairing and maintaining the home)	"When I scrub the floor, I notice now I find that my knee hurts. Maybe this is getting older" (Housekeeping)	She is no longer able to climb on a chair or get down on the floor so many home cleaning tasks have become difficult. (Housekeeping)
Shopping and Finances	He is unable to read most printed store receipts, so he always asks someone to read it aloud and keeps a copy to review at home with his magnifier (Paying and signing for things)	No challenges mentioned.	She often has to wait to use the handicap dressing room because "everyone wants it." (Going shopping in-person)
Transportation	"I leave that up to the drivers. I don't try to plan a trip and decide what roads I want to be on". He is no longer able to drive due to progressive vision loss and the number of medications he is taking. (Wayfinding)	She nearly missed a flight because they she was unaware of a gate change announcement made over the intercom. "I just wish that they would make those announcements on some kind of visual display, but you never see that." (Travel)	"There are times were I just can't go where I want to because the vehicle we are using isn't really accessible. (Getting a ride from others)
Managing Your Health	He is unable to read prescription labels, so relies on wife to set up containers. "After having brain surgery last year, my medication went from 6 or 8 pills a day to over 25 pills a day... the hardest part is remembering to do it in the proper time period" (Managing medications)	Her doctor's office provides Video Relay Interpreting (VRI), but sometimes there are connection issues and it is hard to see the interpreter if the screen is blurry. One visit, she stopped using the VRI and instead tried to communicate with the doctor by writing and doing a thumbs-up or thumbs-down. (Going to healthcare provider appointments)	"I would like some help in managing the pills. Sometimes I forget. Even though I'm using a checklist and all that, I'm just not sure of myself. I have to check my blood sugar eight or ten times a day." (Managing medications)
Basic Daily Living Activities	"I'm able to shave. I'm able to brush my teeth. I'm able to do those things but with my memory, sometimes I forget that I didn't do it. (Grooming)	Sometimes she gets vertigo and loses her balance. (Moving around the home)	"I injured one of my legs worse, and had to use the scooter to get into the bedroom and that took planning. I had to get a longer ramp installed. (Movement around the home).

ACKNOWLEDGMENT

This research was supported by a grant from the National Institute on Disability, Independent Living, and Rehabilitation Research (Department of Health & Human Services, Administration for Community Living) Grant 90RE5016-01-00 under the auspices of the Rehabilitation and Engineering Research Center on Technologies to Support Successful Aging with Disability (RERC TechSAge; www.techsage.gatech.edu).

REFERENCES

[1] W. He, and L. Larsen, U.S. Census Bureau, "Older Americans With a Disability: 2008–2012". American Community Survey Reports, ACS-29, U.S. Government Printing Office, Washington, DC, 2014.

[2] M. Putnam, I. R. Molton, A. R. Truitt, A. E. Smith, and M. P. Jensen, "Measures of aging with disability in U.S. secondary datasets: Results of a scoping review," Disability and Health Journal, 9, pp. 5–10, 2016. doi:10.1016/j.dhjo.2015.07.002

[3] L. M. Verbrugge, and L. Yang, "Aging with disability and disability with aging," Journal of Disability Policy Studies, 12, pp. 253–267, 2002. doi:10.1177/104420730201200405

[4] M. P. LePlante, "Key goals and indicators for successful ageing of adults with early onset disability," Disability and Health Journal, 7, pp. 44–50, 2014. doi:10.1016/j.dhjo.2013.08.005

[5] E. M. Agree, "The potential for technology to enhance independence for those aging with a disability," Disability and Health Journal, 7(1 Suppl), pp. 33–39, 2014. doi:10.1016/j.dhjo.2013.09.004

[6] K. C. Preusse, E. T. Gonzalez, J. L. Singleton, T. L. Mitzner, and W. A. Rogers, "Understanding the needs of individuals ageing with impairment," Int. J. Human Factors and Ergonomics Vol. 4, No. 2, pp. 144-168, 2016.

[7] P. B. Baltes, "On the incomplete architecture of human ontogeny. Selection, optimization, and compensation as foundation of developmental theory," The American Psychologist, 52, pp. 366–380, 1997. doi:10.1037//0003-066x.52.4.366

[8] C. N. Harrington, T. L. Mitzner, and W. A. Rogers, "Understanding the role of technology for meeting the support needs of older adults in the USA with functional limitations," Gerontechnology, Vol. 14, No. 1, pp. 21–31, 2015.

Design Criteria to Advance Technologies for the Aging Population

Claudia B. Rebola
Industrial Design, School of Design
University of Cincinnati
Cincinnati, OH USA
claudia.rebola@uc.edu

***Abstract*—Design and technology can have a significant impact on the aging with disability population, empowering these individuals to sustain independence, maintain health, engage safely in basic activities at home/community, and fully participate in society. Even though a large number of resources exist, there is a need to increase knowledge, practice, and availability of universal design for the aging with disability population. A competition can be an effective way to tap into a rich, diverse and collective design intelligence to address these issues. The TechSAge Design Competition was launched to inspire talented designers to develop innovative technology-enabled design solutions. As part of the competition, judging criteria were framed through universal design to guide contestants in the design of technologies. This included: independence, integration, implementation, inspiration, and progression. This paper discusses the judging as a mechanism to promote effective universal design practices for the aging with disability population, as well as presents examples of competition entries reflecting the design criteria.**

Keywords-Design Criteria; Design for Aging; Technologies for Aging; Competition.

I. Introduction

User-centered design approaches have been dominating the creative disciplines in order to design products that better serve users [1]. IDEO, a global design company, was one of the pioneers in harnessing the power of methods to develop a more critical, nuanced and responsive design process [2]. Since then, a plethora of methods has emerged in response to better understanding user needs, especially participatory design methods aimed at involving the targeted user in the design process for meeting the needs of the stakeholders [3]–[6]. While the aforementioned methods are effective for better identifying user requirements, usability, and adoption, they still challenge the impact on design practices as it relates to users with varied abilities such as older adults. Aside from methods, designing for older adults requires focused expertise, considerations, and principles for bringing about effective solutions for the population. There are a number of sources aimed at giving easily accessible information as a primer for designing for older adults. Fisk et al. offer a practical introduction to human factors and older adults by illustrating practical translations of scientific data into design applications [7]. Similarly, Universal Design principles provide guidance for designing products and environments involving the consideration of the human factors across populations of varied abilities [8]. Universal Design holds the promise to design products and environments to be usable by all people, to the greatest extent possible, without the need for adaptation or specialized design [9][10].

While Universal Design principles are an invaluable guide to better design products for older adults, there is still the need to better educate audiences for the successful implementation, especially when designing new technologies [11]. There is a need to collectively position the principles by reformulating how they are presented and communicated. The goal is to set forward a better mechanism to present the universal design principles embedded in practice.

A competition can be an effective way to tap into a rich, diverse and collective design intelligence to address the current needs of our older adults. Moreover, it can be a venue to effectively address the implementation of Universal Design principles in the design process. This paper discusses the guiding criteria for the TechSAge Design Competition built on the Universal Design principles [12]. As a result, the competition aids in not only identifying exemplary practices in design for aging but mainly as a platform to educate and encourage communities of interest to solve the problems the aging population face.

The paper is structured as follows. Section II presents Universal Design competitions while Section III introduces the TechSAge Design Competition mission. Section IV describes the application areas for designing technologies for the older adult population. Section V describes the criteria for guiding the design. Lastly, Section VI presents the exemplars resulting from the competition followed by concluding thoughts about the design competition for framing Universal Design principles for advancing technologies to support a healthy aging for all.

II. Universal Design Competitions

There are a number of Universal Design Competitions that encourage students to design products for people with varied abilities. University of Southern California has been hosting since 2014 the annual Morton Kesten Universal Design Competition in order to create an opportunity for students across the United States to develop universally-designed spaces and products. The competition is developed in association with the Morton Kesten Summit, which is held every two years featuring the latest developments in aging-in-place efforts by organizations and professionals across the country [13]. The competition is framed following the principles of Universal Design [8]. It challenges students to create an innovative design using the principles of Universal

Design that support aging-in-place in one of two areas: Space: a) re-conceptualizing an existing kitchen/bath space; or b) creating a brand-new kitchen/bath space; or Product: developing a product/prototype that embraces and utilizes the ideas and principles of Universal Design for use at home. While the applicants submit a visual presentation along with a description and explanation for the process, judges use the criteria of: 1-having done market research; 2-integrating aesthetic appeal with function; 3- addressing feasibility and cost-effectiveness; 4-being environmentally friendly; 5-describing how it supports aging in place; and most important, 6- showcasing the exercise of the universal design principles.

There is also the Universal Design Grand Challenge (UDGC) in partnership with the National Disability Authority [14]. The competition has also been running since 2014 with the goal of promoting and awarding excellence in student projects that feature solutions that work for everyone. They offer applicants the option of entering into three categories: 1- Information and Communication Technology; 2- Built Environments; and 3- Products and Services. The main criterion for success in the competition is to see products designed using the Principles of Universal Design, with user feedback at the heart of the design process [8]. The competition emphasizes that the goal is not aimed at submitting solutions for disabled people or assistive technology but designing solutions for all. As a requirement, contestants need to be in their final two years of study, postgraduate students and recent graduates enter their best project. Via the website, the competition provides contestants with information on the principles, success stories, and other online resources related to universal design.

While both competition sites offer resources for understanding the principles and other relevant literature for the topic, contestants are left unguided with a set of principles not linked to measurable outcomes other than the principles alone. Though one of the competitions offer entry categories, the openness of application areas may also be limiting for educating contestants about Universal Design. While universal design aims at designing products for all, there is a need to understand needs and provide guidance on the implementation of the principles as it relates to populations.

The Stanford Center on Longevity Design Challenge offers cash prizes and free entrepreneur mentorship in a competition open to all university students around the world who want to design products and services for optimizing long life for us all [15]. While the challenge topics change every year, they provide focus areas related to promoting habits that improve the quality of life for individuals across the lifespan for guiding design creativity. For example, the latest challenge focused on three areas: 1- Healthy Living; 2- Social Engagement; and 3- Financial Security. The main differentiating factor about this competition is its mentorship approach through the two-phase design. Semifinalists are provided with mentorship to further develop the products and services concepts. The contestants then compete with developed ideas for grand prizes and places. While the aim of the competition is to *design for all*, their judging criteria is focused on: 1- Alignment with Challenge Topic; 2- Potential for Impact; 3- Originality; 4- Probability of Implementation; and 5- Economic Viability. As the center states, the best designs usually are the ones that are innovative/novel, engaging, practical, scalable, inexpensive and readily understood, in which user testing of designs has been a critical step for past winners. While this competition guides contestants well in the application areas and measurable success outcomes for a specific population—older adults, it lacks the integration of Universal Design principles for guiding the successful design of products and services for the population.

Addressing the aforementioned limitations and combining the properties of these three competitions, it brings about an opportunity to develop a unique competition mechanism to educate, guide and mentor students in the successful implementation of Universal Design principles linked to the aging population. The next section describes in detail the design of the TechSAge Design Competition.

III. TechSAge Competition

The TechSAge Design Competition is developed to inspire talented designers to bring about innovative technology-enabled design solutions for the aging population [12]. The competition is designed to be a two-phase submission system.

Phase I focuses on the conceptualization of the designs. Phase II focuses on further developing the design through prototyping, testing and co-designing while incorporating feedback from experts in the field. Phase II of the competition allows mentorship though feedback and partnerships. The competition links contestants with varied experts in the topics of universal design, gerontology, human factors, human-computer interaction, to mention a few through different sectors ranging from researchers to practitioners.

The goals of deploying the competition are not only to ignite the design of products, services, and systems for the older adult population but to guide, educate and train international younger generations engaged in effectively designing technologies for aging with disability. More specifically, the competition is framed within the missions:

To support people with chronic conditions and long-term impairments who are at risk of disability or increased disability due to comorbid age-related losses;

By empowering these individuals to sustain independence; maintain health; engage safely in basic activities at home and in the community, and fully participate in society;

Through increasing knowledge about, availability of, and access to effective, universally-designed technologies.

IV. Areas of Design for Aging

Through the competition, contestants are given categories for entering their designs. The categories reflect the contemporary practices of design across sectors, academia, and industry, responding to the needs of healthy aging [11]. As such, contestants can opt to submit in four different areas: 1- Health at Home; 2- Social Connectedness; 3- Active Lifestyle; and 4- Community mobility, as follows:

- *Health in the Home:*

  This category is focused on proposing designed technology solutions for the home environment that support health and healthy activities in support to the healthcare system.

- *Social Connectedness:*

  This category is focused on proposing designed technology solutions to encourage communication, connectedness with people and social activities.

- *Active Lifestyle:*

  This category is focused on proposing designed technology solutions to promote physical and cognitive activities, and how activities can promote healthy lifestyles.

- *Community Mobility:*

  This category is focused on proposing designed technology solutions to facilitate access to activities and/or locations.

V. DESIGN CRITERIA

Contestants are given resources in the areas of resources for understanding topics on design, universal design, aging, and disability. While the resources play a significant role in helping contestants in designing their products, services or experiences for the population, the competition judging criteria play a significant role. The criteria were developed through an iterative process of questioning the limitations of the Universal Design principles as they are applied to the aging population with disability. The Universal Design Principles are embedded as enablers in each criterion. The results are five criteria for advancing the Universal Design principles: 1- Independence; 2- Integration; 3- Implementation; 4- Inspiration; and 5- Progression (see Table I). These criteria are used as an evaluation mechanism that guides the designs. The criteria are explained in the next subsections.

TABLE I. DESIGN CRITERIA

Design Criteria To Advance Technologies for the Aging Population	
Independence **Integration** **Implementation** **Inspiration** **Progression**	Universal Design Principles *1: Equitable Use.* *2: Flexibility in Use.* *3: Simple and Intuitive Use.* *4: Perceptible Information.* *5: Tolerance for Error.* *6: Low Physical Effort.* *7: Size and Space for Approach and Use.*

A. Independence

The focus of setting this criterion is to guide contestants in proposing products and/or systems to empower older adults to take action in their lives. The goal is to overcome the concept of "taking care of" or "doing things for" and enabling older adults to take initiative, take care of and do things for their lives.

B. Integration

The focus of setting this criterion is to guide contestants in proposing products and/or systems to build intergenerational, supported and connected communities. The goal is to develop bottom-up approaches across generations that can help older adults have access to a community of care.

C. Implementation

The focus of setting this criterion is to guide contestants in proposing products and/or systems to have a successful effect and longevity in the aging population. The goal is to develop solutions that are feasible for implementation in the near future and more importantly, sustainable from the point of view of self-maintaining.

D. Inspiration

The focus of setting this criterion is to guide contestants in proposing products and/or systems that are forward thinking and enablers. The goal is to celebrate the aging populating with creative, attractive and pervasive solutions that avoid physical, visual or experiential segregation.

E. Progression

The focus of setting this criterion is to guide contestants in proposing products and/or systems that allow positive growth. The goal is to develop solutions that grow with the aging population and inspire them to do more and be more.

VI. COMPETITION ENTRIES AND RESULTS

Two competitions were deployed since the proposed design. This section reports the results from the first two years of the TechSAge Design Competition.

For the entries, contestants were asked to submit detailed documentation of the concept for Phase I which included conceptual thinking, motivation and concept generation, different views of 3D representation, solutions described in use (i.e. storyboard/scenario), material/electronics specifications, and an implementation plan noting its feasibility/cost. For Phase II, contestants were required to resubmit updated documentations a from Phase I but more importantly, adding descriptions of the technology components, and development of a testing prototype that is validated through user studies with older adults. Phase II also required an additional submission of a poster and video documentary.

The entries were judged in both phases with the same on the proposed criteria. Phase I judging was online, while Phase II judging was performed via an exhibition (see Figure 1).

Figure 1. Jury evaluating Phase II of the comeptition.

A. First TechSAge Design Comeptition

For the first competition, submissions were distributed across categories as follows: Health at Home category received 39% of the total entries; Active Lifestyle category received 30% of the total entries; Social Connectedness category received 22% of the total entries; and Community Mobility category received 9% of the total entries. The distribution reveals an increased interest among contestants in designing health technologies for the home as opposed to a reduced interest in designing technologies that enable mobility for older adults aging with a disability. In the first year of the competition, up to three semifinalists for each category were selected to move to Phase II of the competition. Contestants received financial support to further develop their concepts into working testable prototypes.

The 1st place was awarded to *Dex*, a smart foot care system designed to promote exercise and health management for people with diabetes (see Figure 2). The Dex system features pressure sensitive shoe insoles that interact with a smartphone, enabling the user to monitor their foot pressure and play various exergames.

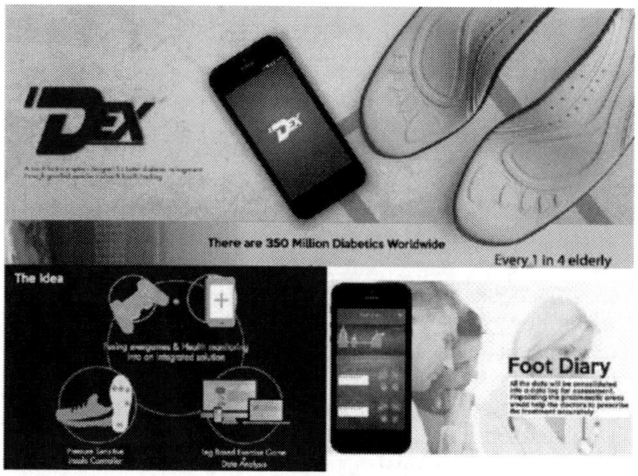

Figure 2. Dex Smart Sole System.

CommuniTea, a connected scheduling board for older adults, was awarded second place (see Figure 3). The peg board tablet offers a simple, connected way for people to plan meeting arrangements based on their activities, skills and interests [16]. The CommuniTea concept exemplifies well the criteria of Progression and Inspiration.

An airport wayfinding app for senior travelers, known as *GatePal*, took third place (see Figure 4). GatePal provides step-by-step instructions for users to successfully navigate the airport and complete key tasks, from checking in, locating their gate, and finding their luggage [17]. GatePal is universally designed so that older adults with different functional abilities are able to use this app at their own pace and in their preferred way.

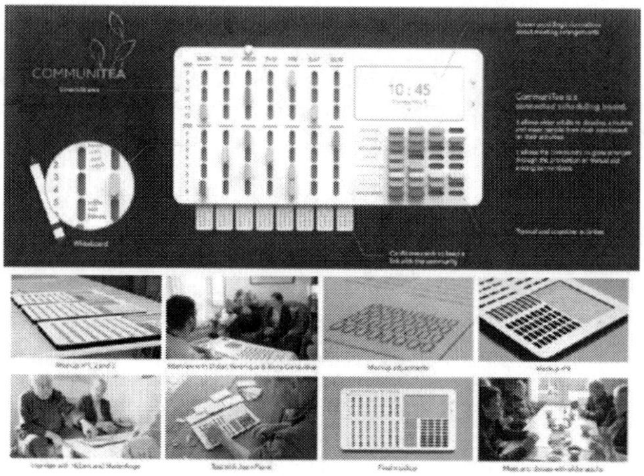

Figure 3. CommuniTea Interctive Scheduling Board.

Figure 4. GatePal Navigation System.

While all winning entries demonstrate well all the criteria, the Dex concept exemplifies well the criteria of Independence and Integration; the CommuniTea concept exemplifies well the criteria of Progression and Inspiration; and the GatePal concept exemplifies well the criteria of Implementation, Integration and Independence.

B. Second TechSAge Design Comeptition

For the second competition, submissions were distributed across categories as follows: Social Connectedness category received 36% of the total entries; Active Lifestyle category received 29% of the total entries; Health at Home category received 21% of the total entries; and Community Mobility category received 14% of the total entries. Compared to the previous year, Active Lifestyle maintained the lead of interest while Health at Home decreased two positions down in interest, switching places with Social Connectedness in the lead. Whereas, Community Mobility remained as the least interest category.

Overall, combining results from the two competitions, students responding to the population needs results in positioning Health at Home in the first place, Social Connectedness in the second place, Active Lifestyle in the third place and Community Mobility last (see Figure 5). With these results, there is an opportunity to increase awareness and resources to better promote the development of design and technologies focusing on mobility.

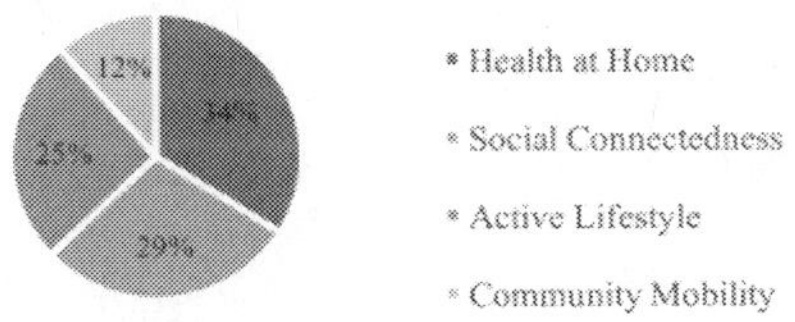

Figure 5. TechSAge Competition Submissions Distribution Across Categories.

With entries representing a large number of international institutions, the jury selected *Releaf* not only as the top score in the Active Lifestyle category but also awarded the First Place Prize in the second TechSAge Design Competition (see Figure 6) [18]. Releaf was created with the goal of increasing the opportunity for active gardening for seniors considering the barriers such as lost grip strength. The design featured a robotic glove that uses cables and servos wired to a sensor controlled by the pinky to engage and disengage the active assistance when gripping tools.

Project *Nettle* won top place in the Social Connectedness category (see Figure 7). The project focuses on designing interfaces which do not require glowing screens or lengthy training to comprehend but instead working naturally with the way information is absorbed by the senses and physically tying into familiar forms. Nettle is an intuitive screen less interface for community connection consisting of a teapot and mug and employing the beloved rituals of making tea. Unlike products for teleconferencing distant family members, Nettle offers a safe and fun way to incorporate social outreach into everyday routines, fostering resilient community ties over time.

Project "MODU" won top category *Health at Home*. MODU is a universal multipurpose, customizable and modular assistive system designed to assist those who face challenges in mobility.

Figure 6. Releaf Robotic Gradening Glove.

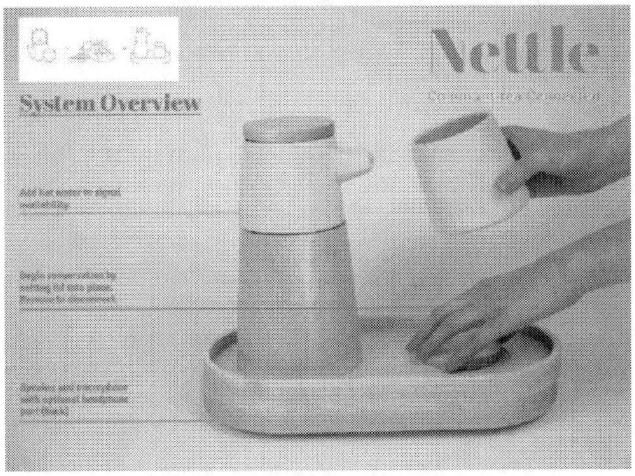

Figure 7. Nettle Communication Device.

VII. CONCLUSION

Building on the strengths of Universal Design, this paper discussed the TechSAge Design Competition, launched to inspire talented designers to develop innovative technology-enabled design solutions. The competition features a mechanism to implement Universal Design training on a broad basis. At the application area, it also generates international awareness and understanding of aging with disability and encourage contestants in generating new technologies for successful aging with disability. For training and awareness, the competition advances criteria for evaluating successful technologies for the older adult population aging with disability. The criteria are: independence, integration, implementation, inspiration, and progression. This paper serves an attempt to provide organized criteria that the design for aging with disability community and related disciplines can adopt for advancing technologies to improve the lives of older adult aging with disability. The significance of this paper is to introduce approaches that better guide the design of products, technologies and/or services when designing for the older adults. Through this contest, students get to understand that design activities cannot be separated from abilities; design IS ability, and creative technologies can emerge from looking at disabilities as a source of inspiration for great *designs for all*.

ACKNOWLEDGMENT

The contents of this paper were developed under a grant from the National Institute on Disability, Independent Living, and Rehabilitation Research (NIDILRR grant number 90RE5016-01-00) under the auspices of the Rehabilitation and Engineering Research Center on Technologies to Support Successful Aging with Disability (TechSAge; www.techsage.gatech.edu). NIDILRR is a Center within the Administration for Community Living (ACL), Department of Health and Human Services (HHS). The contents of this paper do not necessarily represent the policy of NIDILRR, ACL, or HHS, and you should not assume endorsement by the Federal Government.

REFERENCES

[1] IDEO, *Human-Centered Design Toolkit: An Open-Source Toolkit to Inspire New Solutions in the Developing World*, 2 edition. IDEO, 2011.

[2] IDEO [Online]. Available: https://www.ideo.com. [Accessed: 05-Mar-2018].

[3] B. Hanington and B. Martin, *Universal Methods of Design: 100 Ways to Research Complex Problems, Develop Innovative Ideas, and Design Effective Solutions*, 58480th edition. Beverly, MA: Rockport Publishers, 2012.

[4] L. Sanders and P. J. Stappers, *Convivial Toolbox: Generative Research for the Front End of Design*. Amsterdam: BIS Publishers, 2013.

[5] E. B.-N. Sanders, E. Brandt, and T. Binder, "A Framework for Organizing the Tools and Techniques of Participatory Design," in Proceedings of the 11th Biennial Participatory Design Conference, New York, NY, USA, 2010, pp. 195–198.

[6] V. Kumar, *101 Design Methods: A Structured Approach for Driving Innovation in Your Organization*, 1 edition. Hoboken, N.J: Wiley, 2012.

[7] A. D. Fisk, W. A. Rogers, N. Charness, S. J. Czaja, and J. Sharit, *Designing for Older Adults: Principles and Creative Human Factors Approaches, Second Edition*, 2 edition. Boca Raton: CRC Press, 2009.

[8] Center for Universal Design, "The Principles of Universal Design." [Online] Available: https://projects.ncsu.edu/ncsu/design/cud/about_ud/udprinciples.htm. [Accessed: 28-Feb-2018].

[9] W. Lidwell, K. Holden, and J. Butler, *Universal Principles of Design, Revised and Updated: 125 Ways to Enhance Usability, Influence Perception, Increase Appeal, Make Better Design Decisions*. Rockport Publishers, 2010.

[10] J. A. Sanford, Universal Design as a Rehabilitation Strategy: Design for the Ages, 1 edition. New York: Springer Publishing Company, 2012.

[11] C. B. Rebola, *Designed Technologies for Healthy Aging*. Morgan & Claypool Publishers, 2015.

[12] TechSAge Design Competition [Online]. Available: http://techsagecompetition.com. [Accessed: 05-Mar-2018].

[13] USC Leonard Davis School of Gerontology, "Morton Kesten Universal Design Competition." [Online]. Available: http://gero.usc.edu/udcompetition/. [Accessed: 27-Feb-2018].

[14] Centre for Excellence in Universal Design, "Universal Design Grand Challenge Student Awards." [Online]. Available: http://universaldesign.ie/Awards/Student-Awards/. [Accessed: 27-Feb-2018].

[15] Standford Center of Longevity, "Design Challenge." [Online]. Available: http://longevity.stanford.edu/design-challenge-2017-18/. [Accessed: 28-Feb-2018].

[16] P. Giret, "CommuniTea." [Online]. Available: http://paulingiret.com/communitea. [Accessed: 28-Feb-2018].

[17] Y. E. Liu, C. Harrington, S. Melgen, and J. A. Sanford, "GatePal – Universal Design for Airport Navigation to Allow Departing Travellers to Stay Informed," in Universal Access in Human-Computer Interaction. Users and Context Diversity, Cham, 2016, pp. 586–594.

[18] J. Chang, "Releaf Glove." [Online]. Available: http://justinchangdesign.com/?p=1345 [Accessed: 5-Mar-2018].

Universally Designed mHealth App for Individuals Aging with Multiple Sclerosis

Ljilja Ruzic, Harshal P. Mahajan, and Jon A. Sanford
The Center for Assistive Technology and Environmental Access (CATEA)
Georgia Institute of Technology
Atlanta, GA, USA
e-mail: ljilja@gatech.edu, harshal.mahajan@design.gatech.edu, jon.sanford@design.gatech.edu

Abstract—**Multiple Sclerosis (MS) presents with chronic symptoms that share many of the functional limitations associated with aging. Additionally, following the period of five years post-diagnosis a large number of individuals diagnosed with MS experience a major decline in their abilities due to the progression of MS. Consequently, they need to learn how to cope with the functional limitations caused by the disease and in addition to those caused by aging. These individuals have to manage the effects of the disease on their lives every day. mHealth apps provide potential support for disease self-management. However, the number of mobile apps design specifically for individuals with MS is inadequate. Additionally, there is no evidence that utility and usability of these current consumer mobile apps were tested with their target population. This research paper describes the design of the mHealth app MS Assistant, an evidence-based app that provides the daily support and self-management of the disease to individuals aging with MS. It was developed based on the Universal Design Mobile Interface Guidelines, UDMIG v.2.1 and the results of the two previous studies that assessed the health and wellness self-management needs in individuals with MS and tested the usability of current mHealth apps. The paper presents an app refinement based on the suggestions of the expert reviewers who tested the effectiveness of the implementation of the UDMIG v.2.1 in the app design and provided possible recommendations for its redesign.**

Keywords-mHealth apps; multiple sclerosis; aging with disabilities; universal design.

I. INTRODUCTION

The size of the population aging with disabilities is growing [1][2]. Individuals aging with Multiple Sclerosis (MS) are one example of this population. MS is an inflammatory disorder of the Central Nervous System (CNS). This chronic and progressive disease is affecting around 400,000 individuals in the US and 2.5 million people worldwide, with approximately 10,000 newly diagnosed cases of MS annually [3]. It is one of the most common causes of disability in young adults.

MS presents with chronic symptoms that share many of the functional limitations associated with aging (e.g., fatigue, problems with balance, weakness, vision impairments, cognitive impairment, pain, sleep disorders, bowel and bladder dysfunction) [4]-[7]. Additionally, a large number of people diagnosed with MS experience a major decline in their abilities due to the progression of MS after five years post-diagnosis [8]. Consequently, these individuals need to learn how to cope with the functional limitations caused by the disease and in addition to those caused by aging.

MS has significant consequences on patients' Quality of Life (QOL) [9][10]. Individuals with MS experience a large number of physical, cognitive and emotional challenges on a daily basis [11][12]. As the most common symptoms in people with MS, fatigue, functional disability, and cognitive impairment have an enormous impact on a person's health-related QOL [13]. As a result, these individuals have to manage the effects of the disease on their lives every day. More specifically, they need a continuous disease, symptom, and medication management, coupled with education and effective strategies for addressing the exacerbations (i.e., a worsening of old symptoms or an onset of new symptoms for at least 24 hours, also called a relapse) [12].

mHealth apps provide potential support for disease self-management [14]. These health and wellness self-monitoring mobile apps can assist with the daily organization of health and wellness, communication with the healthcare providers, and patient education. The majority of individuals diagnosed with MS already use modern communication technology regularly [15]. They accepted and adopted new forms of electronic communication (e.g., mobile app, text messaging, email, and website) for exchanging information about MS with the health care providers for the management of MS and scheduling appointments.

However, the number of mobile applications designed specifically for the people with MS is inadequate. Additionally, there is no evidence that utility and usability of these consumer mobile apps were tested with their target population.

This paper describes the design of the mHealth app MS Assistant, an evidence-based app that provides individuals aging with MS with the daily support and self-management of their disease [16]. It was developed based on the Universal Design Mobile Interface Guidelines, UDMIG v.2.1 [17]-[20] and the results of the two previous studies [16][18] that assessed the health and wellness self-management needs in individuals with MS and tested the usability of current mHealth apps. The paper presents an app refinement based on the suggestions of the expert reviewers who tested the effectiveness of the implementation of the UDMIG v.2.1 in the app design and provided possible recommendations for its redesign.

This paper is organized into six sections. Section II reviews the related work about technological support for people with MS and other chronic conditions that share similar symptoms with MS. Section III describes the initial design of MS Assistant. Section IV summarizes the evaluation of the effectiveness of implementing UDMIG v.2.1 in the design of the app through an expert review. Section V presents the refinement of MS Assistant based on the recommendations of the expert reviewers. Section VI provides a conclusion and proposes future work.

II. Related Work

The majority of individuals with MS use modern communication technology regularly (i.e., personal computer, internet, email, mobile phone) [15]. They have high levels of acceptance for using electronic communication methods for exchanging information with health care providers. Ninety six percent of them possessed mobile phones and older participants used it less frequently. However, there is a lack of relevant previous research on needs and concerns of individuals aging with MS [7] to inform the design of the mHealth apps for this group of end-users.

There are only nine current mobile applications available to this group of users, which primarily focus on providing basic information about latest research, news, and practical tips on health, nutrition, and fitness, self-recording of health status, medication adherence, daily activities, symptoms, mood, and similar, and/or sharing the data with healthcare providers. These nine mobile apps provide only basic functionality that can be found in other health apps for the general population and individuals with other chronic conditions. Multiple Sclerosis Association of America (MSAA) released a mobile phone app for health self-reporting, My MS Manager, for individuals with MS and their caretakers [21]. Similarly, MS self app offers a journal that can be later easily accessed by the user who can share their data with the healthcare team [22]. Another self-reporting app is called MySidekick for MS [23], which also provides medicine reminders and a memory exercise. My MS Conversations provides an interactive group session with experienced virtual patients on selected topics [24]. MS Journal is an injection reminder tool for individuals with MS and their caregivers limited to UK market only [25]. My Multiple Sclerosis Diary [26] is another injection reminder mobile app that offers injection location and time set up. SymTrack was designed as a health self-reporting tool that stores shares the health charts with healthcare providers [27]. Social app MS Buddy [28] pairs individuals with MS with another person with MS to chat daily. MS Attack app [29] helps users learn about MS symptoms, how these present themselves during the MS attack and provides a location of the UT MS Clinic and the Neuro Eye Center.

III. MS Assistant

MS Assistant is an evidence-based app, which provides the health and wellness self-management-based functionality, allows for personalization, assists with medication adherence and other daily tasks with alert and reminder systems, and sends alerts to the caregivers, family members, and healthcare providers in a case of an emergency. Its eight functions were selected based on the findings of a qualitative study [16], which was conducted to identify the specific needs for self-management of health and wellness among people aging with MS and to recognize the opportunities to meet those needs through mobile apps. The functions include diary, reports, MS friends, games, education, goals, vitals, and emergency. In addition, profile and settings were designed to offer personalization and customization. Additionally, MS Assistant was designed using the UDMIG v.2.1, which were prioritized based on the previous study [18] that assessed the usability of the two current mHealth apps for people with MS and one for the general population to provide the recommendations for the design of mobile health and wellness app for individuals with MS.

A. Functionality

Diary provides a comprehensive tool for understanding the disease on a daily basis and over time, and how best to manage it through everyday self-management tasks, such as mood, symptoms, energy level, activity, sleep length and quality, and diet. Reports allows users to compile their health management data into useful reports that can be shared electronically with healthcare providers and caregivers. MS Friends is a social support feature that connects users with other people with MS to share their experiences and everyday challenges. Games features VR games that would enable users to perform real-world activities that they might find challenging. In addition, this feature has cognitive and classic games that help people with MS with cognitive functioning, and physical games, which help them with the balance. Education provides the latest news and research about MS as well as health and wellness tips. Goals enables users to set up their personal health and wellness goals to keep them motivated and inspired. Vitals offers remote health and wellness monitoring through the Bluetooth connected devices, such as blood pressure monitoring devices, scales, sleep and activity trackers (e.g., Fitbit), and similar. Emergency lets users place calls directly to their healthcare providers, caregivers, and 911.

The mHealth app sends alert messages to the caregivers, family members, and/or healthcare providers in a case of an emergency (i.e., when the values of certain vitals go above the threshold, such as blood pressure, self-reported depression, extreme values of the symptoms severity, etc.).

B. Navigation

MS Assistant provides two types of navigation: linear and random access. Linear interaction allows users to go through the pages by making or skipping a selection and pressing the Next button. Users can go through the whole interface in a linear fashion by using the Next and Back buttons on every page, which provides consistency and simplicity. After a selection is made, the Next button takes users to the following page of the interface. When the user taps on any button, the button changes to the selected colored background and white text that visually emphasizes the selection. To change the selection, user can tap the button again to deselect it (Figure 1). Random access allows skipping the options and provides a faster pace of the navigation through the direct selection (Figure 2).

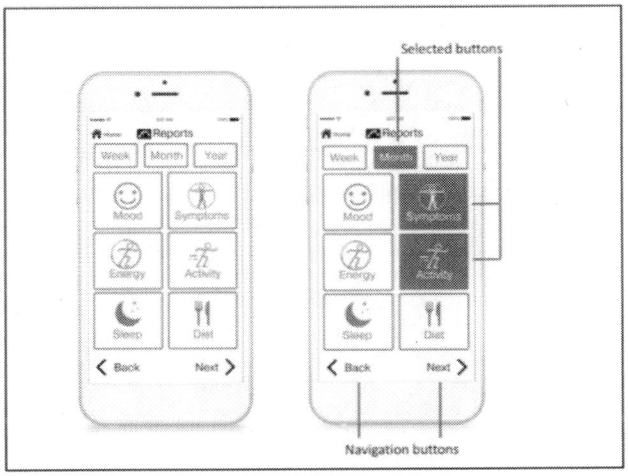

Figure 1. Linear navigation on Reports page.

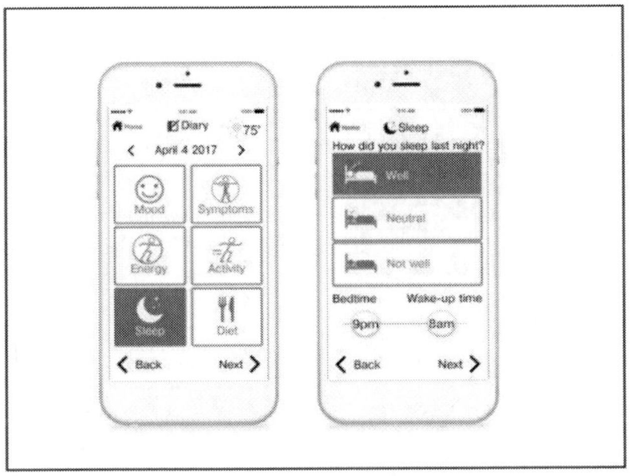

Figure 2. Random access on Diary page.

C. *Design Decisions*

MS Assistant was designed based on the UDMIG v. 2.1 and corresponding design criteria, which has been previously reported [20]. For example, the design goal was one mobile app for all users, rather than accessible design for people with disabilities, and avoidance of specialized design and language (*Same means of use*). Consistent sequences of actions are required in similar situations (*Consistency with expectations*). Complexity is eliminated by having simple screen designs that require a small number of tasks per screen (*Simple and natural use*).

IV. Evaluation of the Effectiveness of Implementing the UDMIG v.2.1

Evaluation of the effectiveness of implementing UDMIG v.2.1 in the design of MS Assistant was conducted with expert reviewers who identified design elements that needed improvement to successfully apply the guidelines and recommend possible refinements [20].

A. *Methods*

Ten researchers and/or designers with experience in aging, accessibility, human-computer interaction, human factors, industrial design, universal design, and/or usability participated in the study. They completed a demographic questionnaire [20], performed directed tasks using the script and MS Assistant without any training or assistance. The script included entering health and wellness data, emailing the reports, calling MS friend, finding virtual reality games, reading the MS news, setting up the weight goal, inputting the blood pressure, calling the healthcare provider, entering the personal information, and increasing the text size [20]. The whole study was audio recorded. Experts then used the UDMIG v.2.1 design criteria questionnaire to rate how well each guideline was implemented, to identify design elements needing improvement, and to provide possible recommendations for their refinement on the 5-point Likert scale where 1 = strongly disagree and 5 = strongly agree with each of the applicable design criteria. Additionally, the audio files during the participants' use of MS Assistant and administration of the talk aloud protocol were analyzed to extract more usability problems they encountered during the interaction with the app.

B. *Results From the UDMIG v.2.1 Design Criteria Questionnaire*

10 participants rated 50 items (i.e., design criteria) on the checklist. The total number of responses was 484, with 16 missing responses that were not used in the data analyses. The mean of all the design criteria ratings per participant was within a range of 3.90 – 4.89. Out of a total of 484 responses, almost 70% (n=332) of the design criteria was rated as 5. An additional one-quarter (n=126) was rated as 4. The lowest rating for any criterion was 2 (n=6) and remaining 20 design criteria were rated as 3. Among the 10 participants, mean ratings ranged from 3.86 – 4.92. The participant with the lowest overall mean rating (M = 3.86) did not give a rating higher than 4 to any individual criterion with 44 rated as 4 and 6 rated as 2 or 3.

C. *Results from the Audio Transcripts*

During the talk-aloud protocol expert reviewers identified usability problems with the interface. Audio transcripts revealed some additional usability problems reported by the participants and the existing problems were reported by a larger number of participants verbally, except in the case of the color contrast and alternative voices in Settings. All usability problems were grouped into the problematic design features and related characteristic so that appropriate design response could be specified.

Main usability problems were labeling of the buttons, use of Next and Back buttons for the linear navigation, design of a number of UI elements, lack of page scrolling with the use of a keyboard, layout of a number of the buttons, certain feature requests, miscategorization of a number of labels, and navigation related to the design of the buttons and pages. For example, problems with the labels for Education, Emergency, Input, and Output buttons were reported by a majority of the participants (Table I). Labeling of the Speech button was reported by 40% of the participants. Additionally, participants commented unfavorably on the use of Next and Back buttons for the linear navigation. However, they understood that the linear navigation using these two buttons might be more usable for the aging population of users. Moreover, they acknowledged that the smart interface and an option to switch from novice to expert user skips this way of the navigation for the more tech-savvy users.

Design of certain UI elements was reported as well. For example, Profile and Settings did not look like buttons, and the slider needed some redesign to half of the participants. Thirty percent of participants reported that Header looked like a button and that certain icons need to be redesigned. Additionally, half of the participants reported that the page scrolling should be present while using the keyboard. Sixty percent of participants reported that the layout of the buttons needed to be changed (e.g., locations of Email Reports and View Reports buttons should be switched). Additionally, 40% of them thought that the spacing between the top buttons (e.g., Manual input button in Vitals, Week, Month, Year buttons in Reports) and the buttons bellow should be increased. Total of 30% of participants thought that after missing to fill out all the fields on one page, the prompt that follows should give them two options. First, it should let them go back to the previous page to fill out the missing content. Alternatively, it should allow them to go to the following page and leave certain fields empty.

There was a number of problems that were found on the audio transcripts, which were not reported on the questionnaire. For example, 60% of participants thought that the app would benefit from the additional features (e.g., a place to specify the body area in Difficulties, the user's current weight with the text "This is what your weight is right now" in the weight goals, a lauder sound feedback with the use of the buttons, etc.). Miscategorization of certain labels was a problem to half of the participants. Additionally, 60% of participants reported problems with navigation due to the lack of direction, page design, and multiple selections.

Moreover, there was a number of problems and related design features and characteristics that were reported by a small number of participants, listed in Table I (i.e., one and two participants).

V. Refinement of MS Assistant

All the design features and related characteristics that needed to be redesigned based on the results of both the UDMIG v.2.1 design criteria questionnaire and audio transcripts were summarized (Table I). The rationale for the design response was to make a design change if in agreement with UDMIG v.2.1, if at least two participants reported the problem, and if the suggestions were not already present in the prototype of MS Assistant. For the number of participants in Table 1, the larger number reported by either the analysis of audio files or the UDMIG v.2.1 checklist was used. This way, the total number of participants reporting a problem was listed.

Dark grey background on the instruction pages was changed into white to provide more contrast against the black and green (i.e., confirmation) text (Figure 3). "Education" was renamed into "Resources", "Emergency" into "Emergency Contacts" (Figure 4), "Energized" (in Mood) into "Excited", "Input" into "Speech Input", "Touch" into "Touch Input", "Output" into "Display and Sound", and "Speech" was replaced with "Voice".

Due to the lack of space on the top navigation bar, name of the app, MS Assistant, was taken out of the Home page and the icons for Profile and Settings were added (Figure 4). The color of the icons for the current state (e.g., Diary, Reports, etc.) was changed from black into the color of that function (e.g., Diary icon in green, Reports icon in blue, etc.). In this way, the icon and the header look like the part of the page background and not like the buttons (Figure 3).

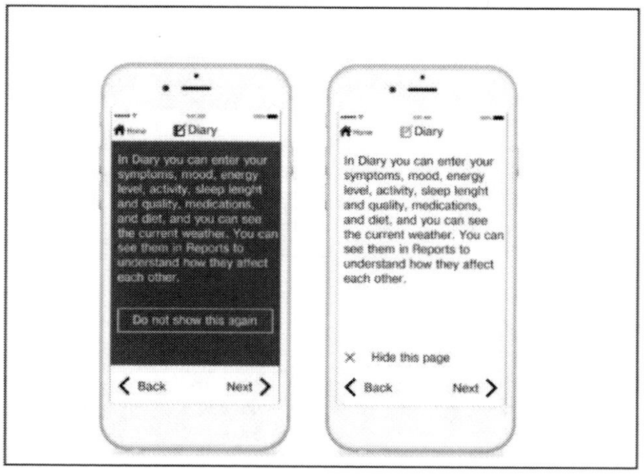

Figure 3. Before (left) and after (right) Diary Instruction page

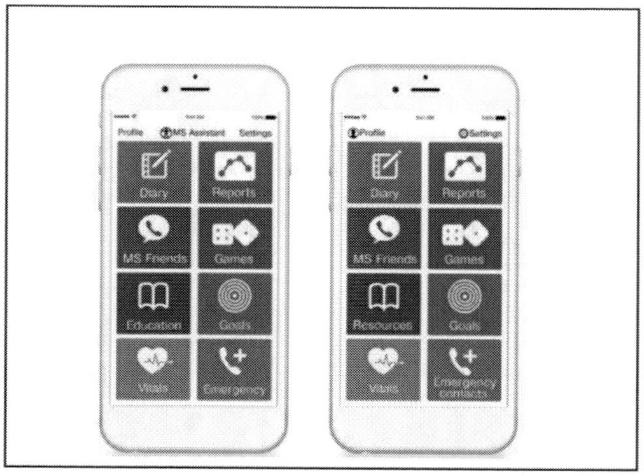

Figure 4. Before (left) and after (right) Home page

TABLE I. DESIGN CHANGES BASED ON THE IDENTIFIED PROBLEMS WITH THE DESIGN FEATURES AND CHARACTERISTICS THROUGH BOTH THE UDMIG V.2.1 DESIGN CRITERIA QUESTIONNAIRE AND AUDIO TRANSCRIPTS

Design Feature and Related Characteristic		**Number of Participants, N**	**Design Response**	**Design Changes**
Background, Contrast		N=3	Increase contrast	Grey was changed into white with black and green text on instruction pages.
Next and Back buttons, Navigation		N=7	No change	No change was made due to the design criteria IC2d. (i.e., Have more than one way to go to different pages while keeping the consistency). Next and Back buttons are typical of linear navigation.
Buttons, Labeling	Education	N=7	Change labeling: Education	"Education" was renamed into "Resources".
	Emergency	N=7	Change labeling: Emergency	"Emergency" was renamed into "Emergency Contacts".
	Energized	N=2	Change labeling: Energized	"Energized" (in Mood) was changed into "Excited".
	Input, Output	N=7	Change labeling: Input, Output	"Input" was renamed into "Speech Input", "Touch" into "Touch Input", and "Output" into "Display and Sound".
	Speech	N=4	Change labeling: Speech	"Speech" was renamed into "Voice".
	News	N=1	No change	No change was made to "News" due to the inconsistency with other button labels within "Resources."
	Diary	N=1	No change	No change was made due to the small number of participnats reporting the problem.
	Do not show this again	N=1	No change	No change was made due to the small number of participnats reporting the problem.
UI elements, design (form and color)	Profile, Settings	N=5	Redesign Profile and Settings buttons	Name of the app, MS Assistant, was taken out of the Home page top navigation bar, and the icons for Profile and Settings were added.
	Header	N=3	Redesign header	Black color of the icons for the current state was changed into the color of that function (e.g., Diary icon in green, Reports icon in blue, etc.).
	Slider	N=5	Redesign slider	Numbers on the slider were placed on the top of it.
	Icons	N=3	Redesign icons	Speech icon was replaced with Output icon, and Input icon with Speech icon. Output icon and Seeing icon (in Difficulties) were redesigned.
	MS type	N=1	No change	No change was made due to problems that drop-down menu causes for people with limited dexterity, similar to the use of the picker.
Settings, Alternative voices		N=3	No change	No changes were made since this prototype included voices within the Settings.
Keyboard, spell check		N=1	Provide spell check w/keyboard	Spell check was provided within the keyboard.
Keyboard, Page scrolling		N=5	Add page scrolling w/keyboard	Page scrolling was added with the use of a keyboard.
Prompt, Content		N=3	Redesign prompt	Prompt was redesigned to inform about the missing data and to allow the navigation to the following page without having to fill out all information.
System, Navigation		N=2	Add text to the first instruction page	Text about the navigation and using Next and Back buttons was added to the first instruction page.
Text, font size		N=2	Increase font size	The font size of the MS News articles was increased.
Buttons, Layout		N=6	Change the layout	View Report button was moved above the Email Report button. Names of the VR games were shortened. The other changes were not made due to the inconsistencies.
Buttons, Haptic feedback		N=3	No change	iPhone 6 does not have the Taptic Engine that provides the vibration.
Buttons, Single tap		N=1	No change	No change was made due to the design criteria IC13a (i.e., Use a single tap throughout the app instead of double-clicking).
Button spacing, Layout		N=6	Increase spacing	Spacing between the top buttons and large buttons bellow was increased.
Feature, Feature request		N=6	Add information about a MS friend	Information about MS Friends was added on the calling page. No other changes were made due to the small number of participants reporting the specific problem (N=1 per problem).
Labels, Miscategorization		N=5	No change	No changes were made due to the small number of participnats reporting the specific problem (N=1 per problem).
Page layout, Lack of consistency		N=2	No change	No change was made to the second page of Reports due to the lack of page space.
Keyboard, On-screen verification		N=1	No change	No change was made since the on-screen verification exists within the input field.
Buttons and pages, Navigation		N=6	No change	No changes were made to the small number of participants reporting the specific problem (N=1 per problem).
Lack of confirmation of an activity, Navigation		N=1	No change	No change was made due to the small number of participants reporting the problem.

Numbers on the slider were placed on the top of it. Speech icon was replaced with Output icon, and Input icon with Speech icon. Output icon and Seeing icon (in Difficulties) were redesigned. Even though only one participant reported that there was no spell check with the use of a keyboard, this general feature was implemented because it is present in a majority of the apps. Page scrolling was added with the use of a keyboard. A prompt was redesigned to inform about the missing data in a way that allows users to go to the following page without having to fill out all information (i.e., "Do you want to fill out the missing information?" with Yes that takes them back to the previous page, and No that takes them to the following page). Text about the navigation (i.e., linear navigation using Next and Back buttons) was added to the first instruction page. The font size of the MS News articles was increased. The layout of the buttons was changed (e.g., View Report button was moved above the Email Report button, and the names of the VR games were shortened). The other layout changes were not made due to the inconsistencies with the page layout. A spacing between the top buttons and large buttons bellow (e.g., Manual entry, and Week, Month, Year buttons) was increased. There was a number of feature requests. For example, additional information about MS Friends is added on the calling page (e.g., friend's interests, MS type, and other information the person wants to share). No changes were made to the other feature requests due to the small number of participants reporting the problem (N=1 per problem).

There were 7 participants reporting a problem with the navigation using Next and Back buttons. However, no change was made due to the design criteria IC2d. (i.e., Have more than one way to go to different pages while keeping the consistency). Next and Back buttons are typical of linear navigation and will be used in the novice user mode only. Additionally, 3 participants did not see that this prototype included alternative voices within the Settings and a problem with it. Similarly, 3 participants reported problems with the lack of the tactile feedback, which was not incorporated because iPhone 6 does not have the Taptic Engine that provides the vibration while tapping the buttons that was included in later versions. The total number of participants reporting the problems with the miscategorization of the labels was 5. However, no changes were made due to the small number of participants reporting the individual problem (N=1 per problem). No change was made to the second page of the Reports due to the lack of page space (N=2). Even though was there was a total of 6 participants who reported a problem with the navigation due to the design of the buttons and pages, no changes were made due to the small number of participants reporting the specific problem (N=1 per problem).

VI. Conclusion and Future Work

The goal of the reported study was to have expert reviewers assess the usability of MS Assistant. The results of the expert review study confirm that MS Assistant effectively implemented UDMIG v.2.1. Most of the participants favorably agreed that the guidelines were implemented appropriately. Ninety percent of the mean values of the participants' ratings were equal to 4 or higher. In addition, there was only a small number of recommendations related to the minor usability problems found in MS Assistant. These design changes were easily implemented in the MS Assistant. Future work will involve usability testing of this mHealth app with the individuals diagnosed with MS at least 5 years ago to understand the overall usability of this mHealth app to determine the effectiveness of UDMIG v.2.1 in producing a universally usable product. This study will help with the analysis of the user-specific differences and preferences towards the individual design features and resulting the design implications.

Acknowledgment

This research was supported by a grant from the National Institute on Disability, Independent Living, and Rehabilitation Research (NIDILRR grant number 90RE5016-01-00) under the auspices of The Rehabilitation Engineering Research Center on Technologies to Support Successful Aging with Disability (RERC TechSAge). NIDILRR is a Center within the Administration for Community Living (ACL), Department of Health and Human Services (HHS).

References

[1] D. Sheets, "Aging with disabilities: ageism and more," Generations, vol. 29, pp. 37-41, 2005.

[2] G. Anderson, "Chronic care: Making the case for ongoing care," Partnership for Solutions, 2010.,

[3] H. Moses, M. Picone, and V. Smith, Clinician's primer on multiple sclerosis: An in-depth overview. CMC, 2008.

[4] M. Stern, "Aging with multiple sclerosis," Physical medicine and rehabilitation clinics of North America, vol. 16, pp. 219-234, 2005.

[5] M. Stern, L. Sorkin, K. Milton, and K. Sperber, "Aging with multiple sclerosis," Physical medicine and rehabilitation clinics of North America, vol. 21, pp. 403-417, 2010.

[6] W. E. Fleming and C. P. Pollak, "Sleep disorders in multiple sclerosis," Seminars in Neurology, pp. 64-68, 2005.

[7] M. Finlayson, "Health and social profile of older adults with MS: Findings from three studies," International Journal of MS Care, vol. 4, pp. 139-151, 2002.

[8] E. E. Gulick, "Symptom and activities of daily living trajectory in multiple sclerosis: a 10-year study," Nursing Research, vol. 47, pp. 137-14, 1998.

[9] P. Rompani and T. Dua, Atlas: Miltiple sclerosis resources in the world 2008. WHO Press, World Health Organization, 2008.

[10] B. Yamout et at., "Predictors of quality of life among multiple sclerosis patients: a comprehensive analysis," European Journal of Neurology, vol. 20, pp. 756-764 , 2013.

[11] A. C. Janssens et al., "Anxiety and depression influence the relation between disability status and quality of life in multiple sclerosis," Multiple Sclerosis Journal, vol. 9, pp. 397-403, 2003.

[12] A. D. Rae-Grant et al., "Self-management in neurological disorders: systematic review of the literature and potential interventions in multiple sclerosis care," Journal of Rehabilitaiton Research and Development, vol. 48, pp. 1087, 2011.

[13] R. Fraser et al., "Self-management for People with Multiple Sclerosis: Report from The First International Consensus Conference, November 15, 2010," International Journal of MS Care, vol. 15, pp. 99-106, 2013.

[14] D. M. Zulman et al., "How can eHealth technology address challenges related to multimorbidity? Perspectives from patients with multiple chronic conditions," Journal of General Internal Medicine, vol. 30, pp. 1063-1070, 2015.

[15] R. Haase, T. Schultheiss, R. Kempcke, K. Thomas, and T. Ziemssen, "Use and acceptance of electronic communication by patients with multiple sclerosis: a multicenter questionnaire study," Journal of Medical Internet Research, vol. 14, pp. e135, 2012.

[16] L. Ruzic and J. A. Sanford, "Needs Assessment: Functional Features in Mobile Health and Wellness Self-Monitoring Applications for People with Multiple Sclerosis," Journal of Healthcare Informatics Research, 2017, in press.

[17] L. Ruzic and J. A. Sanford, "Universal design mobile interface guidelines (UDMIG) for an aging population," in Mobile e-Health, pp. 17-37, 2017.

[18] L. Ruzic and J. A. Sanford, "Usability of mobile consumer applications for individuals aging with Multiple Sclerosis," Proc. 9th International Conference on Universal Access in Human-Computer Interaction (HCII2017), Springer, Jan. 2017, pp. 258-276.

[19] L. Ruzic, C. N. Harrington, and J. A. Sanford, "Design and evaluation of mobile interfaces for an aging population," The Tenth International Conference on Advances in Computer-Human Interactions (ACHI2017), Mar. 2017, pp. 305-309, ISBN: 978-1-61208-538-8

[20] L. Ruzic, C. N. Harrington, and J. A. Sanford, "Universal Design Mobile Interface Guidelines for mobile health and wellness apps for an aging population including people aging with disabilities," International Journal on Advances in Software, vol. 10, pp. 372-384, 2017.

[21] My MS Manager. [Online]. Avalable: https://mymsaa.org/msaa-community/mobile/ [Accessed: 09-Feb-2018].

[22] MS self™, the Multiple Sclerosis Mobile App. [Online]. Avalable: http://www.moveoverms.org/multiple-sclerosis-app-ms-self/ [Accessed: 09-Feb-2018].

[23] MySidekick for MS. [Online]. Avalable: https://www.abovems.com/en_us/home/resources/ms-tools-services/mysidekick-app.html [Accessed: 09-Feb-2018].

[24] My MS Conversations™. [Online]. Avalable: https://play.google.com/store/apps/details?id=com.syandus.ms_patiented_01&hl=en [Accessed: 09-Feb-2018].

[25] MS Journal. [Online]. Avalable: https://itunes.apple.com/us/app/ms-journal/id523663325?mt=8 [Accessed: 09-Feb-2018].

[26] My Multiple Sclerosis Diary. [Online]. Avalable: https://play.google.com/store/apps/details?id=com.appxient.mymsdiary&hl=en [Accessed: 09-Feb-2018].

[27] SymTrack. [Online]. Avalable: http://www.symtrac.com/ [Accessed: 09-Feb-2018].

[28] MS Buddy. [Online]. Avalable: https://play.google.com/store/apps/details?id=com.healthline.msbuddy [Accessed: 09-Feb-2018].

[29] MS Attack. [Online]. Avalable: https://play.google.com/store/apps/details?id=com.cloudninedevelopmentllc.MSAttack&hl=en [Accessed: 09-Feb-2018].

Effects of Advanced Driver Assistance System for Elderly's Safe Transportation

An Analysis Based on Vehicles in Japanese Market Emphasizing the Accessibility Issues of the Advanced Driver Assistance System

Ryosuke Ando,[1] Yasuhiro Mimura,[2] Yasuhide Nishihori,[3] Jia Yang[4]
Research Department
TTRI (Toyota Transportation Research Institute)
Motoshiro-cho 3-17, Toyota, Japan
Email: [1]ando@ttri.or.jp, [2]mimura@ttri.or.jp, [3]nishihori@ttri.or.jp, [4]yang@ttri.or.jp

Abstract—**Japan is a representative super-aging society in the world. Generally, the quality of life is closely related with the elderly's mobility or accessibility to the necessary facilities in daily life. Therefore, how to ensure the sustainability of the elderly's mobility has been a very important issue. In our previous study, we found that driving a car play a very important role in this context. On the other hand, the smart transportation system represented by Advanced Driver Assistance System (ADAS) including Advanced Emergency Braking System (AEBS) is expected to make car driving for the elderly safe and sustainable. This paper uses the data collected in Japan to show that the AEBS is very effective to ensure safe driving for the elderly. Thus, a smart mobility society can be expected in the coming years.**

Keywords- elderly's mobility; traffic safety; Advanced Driver Assistance System (ADAS); Advanced Emergency Braking System (AEBS); diffusion of innovations.

I. Introduction

Japan is well-known as a super-aging society in the world. To make this super-aging society sustainable, the countermeasures securing mobility and accessibility of elderly people have been discussed for a long time not only in Japan but also in the world. Generally, a sustainable public transportation system is considered to be the best solution. However, it is very difficult to achieve this goal successfully. For example, in the Chukyo metropolitan area of Japan where the central city is Nagoya, from 2001 to 2011 (refer to [1]), the number of elderly people being 65 years old and over increased from 1.5 million to 2.0 million (about 1.4 times). Although the public transportation services have been promoted with some incentives for the elderly people, the rail system uses only increased from 158 thousand to 199 thousand (about 1.26 times) and the bus users even decreased from 89 thousand to 88 thousand (0.99 times). In contrast, the automobile users increased from 1.25 million to 2.46 million (about 2.0 times).

Regarding the automobile use of the elderly people, the Japanese government has released the analysis reports many times on the traffic accidents (for example [2]). The fatalities in 24 hours caused by traffic accidents in Japan have been reduced to 3904 persons in 2016 from 6415 persons in 2006. However, the elderly rate is increased from 44.3% in 2006 to 54.8% in 2016. Although we know that the major reason is that the percentage of the elderly people is increasing, more effective countermeasures are required.

As a good solution, autonomous vehicles are rapidly becoming the focus of attention to ensure the accessibility need of all people in the future (such as [3]). However, we should know that there is quite a long way to realize the fully autonomous vehicles society from now ([4] et al.). Therefore, the most important issue goes to how to ensure the safety when the elderly people drive cars by themselves. Here, the safety includes the drivers themselves and the other people.

In the world automobile market, the reality is at the stage of vehicle with Advanced Driver Assistance System (ADAS). And this stage may be considered as a primary stage of the autonomous vehicles society. According to RnR Market Research [5], most major ADAS technologies are attracting less than 10% penetration rates in 2015. However, the penetration rate of the car rear view camera has been kept on a level being higher than 30% since 2014 in Japan. That is, Japan is one of countries with the highest ADAS penetration rates in the world with respect to the automobile sales. Because the ADAS can be thought as a compensation of the physical and mental disability for the elderly drivers, the diffusion of the ADAS may help to reduce the traffic accidents to some extent.

Regarding the effects of ADAS, many previous studies have been implemented worldwide. Davidse [6] denoted that ADAS would extend the older adult's safe mobility as a driver. Winter et al. [7] concluded that Adaptive Cruise Control (ACC) and Highly Automated Driving (HAD) reduce the driving workload and improve the completion of in-vehicle tasks. The research results by Cicchino [8] showed that Forward Collision Warning (FCW), low-speed Autonomous Emergency Braking (AEB) and their combination reduces front-to-rear crash rates by 27%, 43% and 50%, respectively. The study by Son et al. [9] found that age and gender groups affect the performance of in-vehicle technology. In Italy [10], the beeping ADAS was reported having disturbed driving and distract drivers as the negative effect. Again, regarding the negative effects, the study conducted by researchers in the Netherlands [11] tells us that drivers equipped with ADAS cross intersections more often with a critical time-to-collision (TTC). In Canada, the research focused on the comparison between older and younger drivers [12], concluding that advanced in-vehicle signs may increase the frequencies of stopping at intersections with relatively short yellow onsets for both younger and older drivers. As a study regarding aftermarket Collision Avoidance Technology (CAT), a research report [13] was compiled on the basis of surveys in the United States of America (USA). The effectiveness of the lane departure warning system (LDWS) was 76% and that of the FCW was 74.5%.

Taking into account the above background, we report an analysis using the traffic accident data collected in Japan. In this paper, our analysis focuses on the effects of the ADAS for safe mobility, especially with respect to the elderly.

The reminder of the paper is organized as follows: Section II briefly describes the methodology; Section III provides the detailed analysis and results discussion; Section IV gives the conclusion and brings up some suggestions for future research.

II. Methodology

As shown in Figure 1 reported by Ministry of Land, Infrastructure, Transport and Tourism [14], the penetration rates of some representative ADAS applications in Japan are depicted by Advanced Emergency Braking System (AEBS), Lane Keeping Assistance System (LKAS), LDWS and ACC. Among these representative ADAS applications, according to the research report published by TTRI [15], the AEBS is the most popular function, as shown in Figure 2. Therefore, the AEBS is set to be the representative ADAS equipment to be evaluated in this paper.

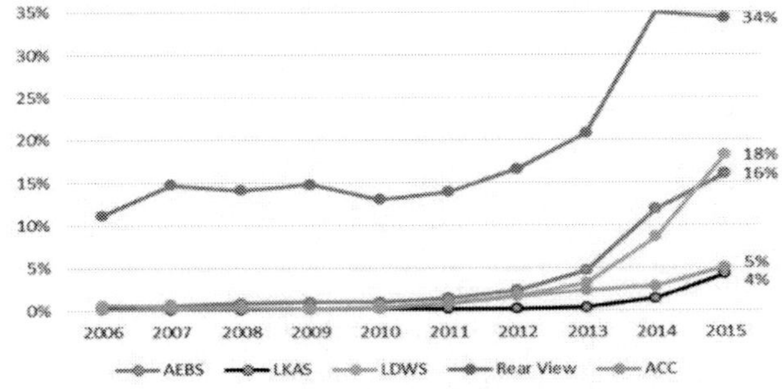

Figure 1. Diffusion of ADAS equipment in Japan [14]

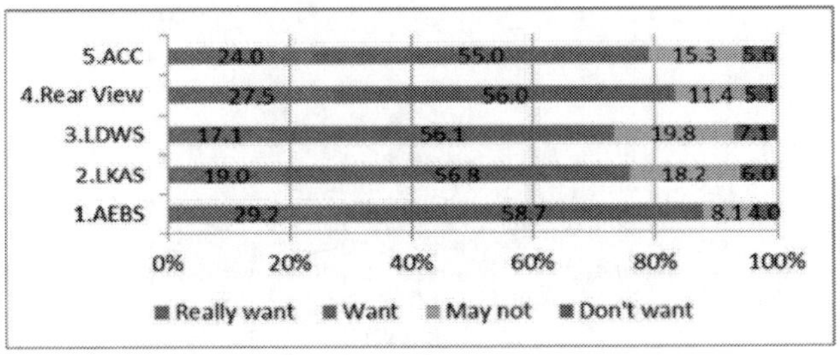

Figure 2. Use Intention of Non-ADAS Users [15].

TABLE I. Equipment Rates of EyeSight [16]

Year	Country		
	Japan	*Europe*	*USA*
2015	83%	96%	31%

In Japan, among all automobile manufacturers, Subaru is the pioneer and introduced the AEBS (named Eyesight) into the vehicle market in 2008. The Eyesight was upgraded twice in the following years, and the updated version 3 released in 2014 has included the ACC, the LDWS and some more functions. We take the AEBS as the target function in this paper by considering that the AEBS is the basic function and has been in market for many years. This long term enables us to collect necessary data to evaluate the effects. In 2015, the percentage of all sold Subaru cars having Eyesight was 83% in the Japan market, as shown in Table 1. Comparing the percentages given in Figure 1, this number was much higher than the average level in Japan. This enables us to evaluate the AEBS by comparing the traffic accidents numbers and rates caused by the Subaru cars and the others. Then, a simulating analysis for the future to secure the safe mobility is given as the conclusion.

III. Analysis and Results

The analysis and discussion can be divided into three steps: A. a general understanding on the possibilities of the ADAS; B. the effects of the ADAS for the elderly drivers; and C. the expected effects to reduce the traffic accident fatalities and the solution for the mobility or the accessibility of the elderly people.

A. General Understanding

Figure 3 is the first comparison between the traffic accidents rate of the newly registered Subaru cars and that caused by other newly registered cars in Japan. Here, the traffic accidents data is the data of all traffic accidents with injuries and it was purchased from the Institute for Traffic Accident Research and Data Analysis (ITARTA) that is entitled to have all traffic accidents data collected in Japan. The traffic accident rates are based on the newly sold/registered vehicles which are collected from Japan Automobile Manufacturers Association, Inc. [17]. From this figure, it is easily understood that the traffic accidents by the newly registered Subaru cars were 1.20 times comparing to other newly registered cars around 2008, but decreased since 2009 and have been only 0.6 times recently. The reason this rate has been flat is because it was also more popular for other cars to be equipped with AEBS starting in 2014, as shown in Figure 1.

In Japan, similarly to the other countries in the world, young drivers under 25 years and elderly drivers 65 years and older are normally considered to be associated with traffic accidents more than other drivers. To analyze the problem, we corrected the traffic accidents occurred in Japan (data source: [18]) and we are showing the results in Figure 4. A comparison between the Subaru cars and other cars is made by the age group, as shown in Figure 5. Here, four age groups are compared. Compared to the traffic accidents in

2008, the traffic accidents by the Subaru cars decreased remarkably since 2012. In contrast, a remarkable decrease of the traffic accidents by other cars starts from 2015. Among the four age groups, the elderly drivers including "64-74" and "75 and older" have shown a steeper decreases compared to young drivers "under 25" and "25-64" years of age.

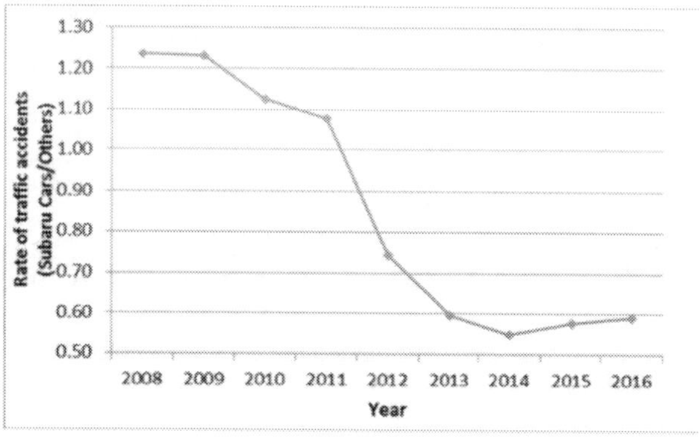

Figure 3. Rates of traffic accidents (Subaru cars/other cars)

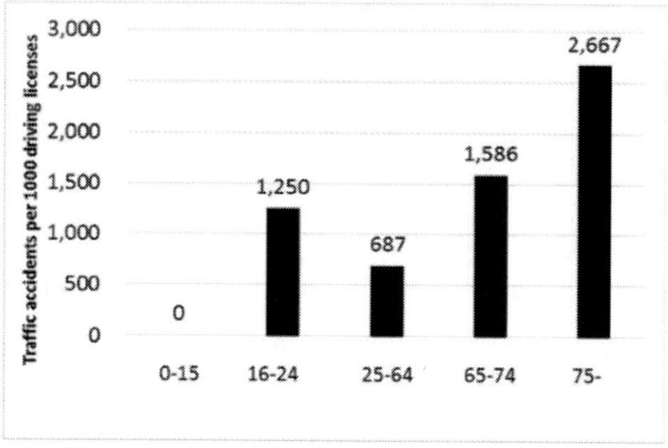

Figure 4. Corrected traffic accidents by age group in Japan

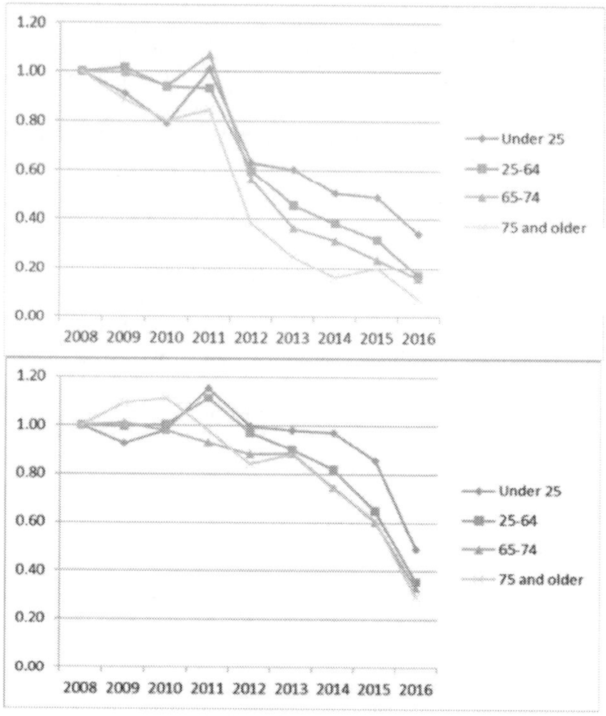

Figure 5. Change of traffic accidents over the years based on driver's age, considering a value of 1.00 in 2008 (top: Subaru cars; bottom: other cars)

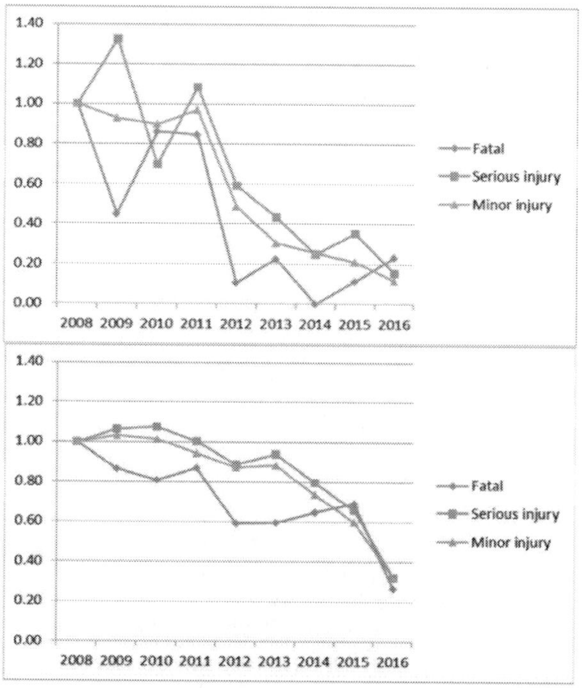

Figure 6. Changes of elderly drivers' accidents over the years in terms of damage, considering a value of 1.00 in 2008 (top: Subaru cars; bottom: other cars)

B. Effects for Elderly Drivers

Regarding the elderly drivers, at first, the effects are compared by the extent of the injury caused by the traffic accidents. As seen in Figure 6, the number of fatal accidents by Subaru cars during the period from 2012 through 2016 is about one-fifth compared to 2008, although there are some irregular changes over the years. Furthermore, by comparing this with the number of fatal accidents by other cars, the noticeable difference during the period from 2012 through 2015 clearly tells us that how much the AEBS contributed to this outcome. Moreover, the 2016 results of both the Subaru cars and others let us know that the AEBS effects are common with all ADAS equipped cars.

Figure 7 summarizes the comparison results by traffic accident classification. Here, P2V stands for "person-to-vehicle", V2V expresses "vehicle-to-vehicle" and "V only" means "vehicle-to-infrastructure" or vehicle alone. From Figure 7, we can know that "vehicle only" accidents with injuries by Subaru cars have been reduced drastically since 2014 when the Eyesight Version 3 was released. Meanwhile, V2V accidents have been reduced in average. Similar results can be seen with other cars in 2016. These results may indicate that the AEBS help the vehicle to recognize large objects such as infrastructures and cars ahead more effectively than the appearance of pedestrians. However, the effects with the "P2V" accidents are becoming conspicuous when many automobile manufacturers equipped the AEBS and other ADAS equipment in 2016.

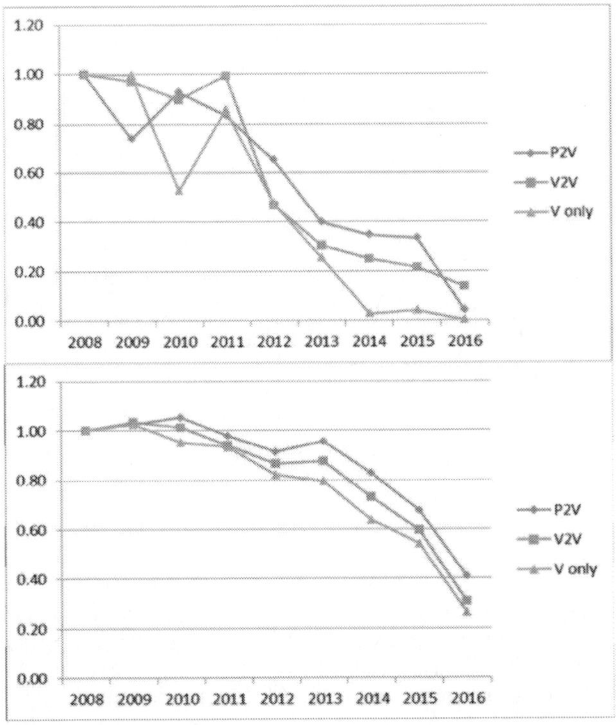

Figure 7. Changes of elderly drivers' accidents over the years in terms of accident classification, considering a value of 1.00 in 2008 (top: Subaru cars; bottom: other cars)

For traffic crash types, the comparison results are depicted in Figure 8. Although there are some irregular movements during 2009 through 2011 for Subaru cars, the remarkable and stable decreasing trends can be seen from 2012 for Subaru cars and from 2014 for other cars. In 2016, all types of traffic accidents have been reduced to less than 40% of those from 2008. Among these crash types, rear end, head-on and crossing crashes have been reduced much more than left turn or right turn crash.

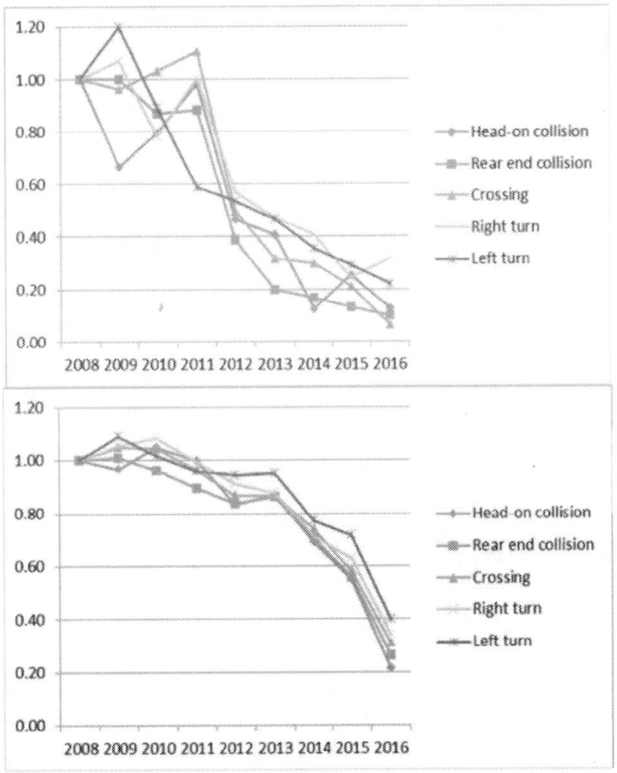

Figure 8. Changes of elderly drivers' accidents over the years in terms of crash type, considering a value of 1.00 in 2008 (top: Subaru cars; bottom: other cars)

Furthermore, the comparison is focused on weather. Figure 9 summarizes changes of the traffic accidents under different weather conditions. Because there is not enough data for Subaru cars in the foggy days, the change of the traffic accidents cannot be expressed here. In addition, a violent fluctuation with the traffic accidents in the snowy days by Subaru cars can be observed. The same can be observed with the traffic accidents in the foggy days by other cars. Therefore, we only want to conclude that the remarkable decreases have been achieved in either the sunny days or the rainy days from Figure 9. Similar to the above analysis, the positive results obtained from 2012 for Subaru cars and from 2014 for other cars support the explanation that these effects are consistent with the diffusion of the AEBS.

Lastly, the comparison is made based on the road environment. The comparison results are shown in Figure 10. As there are some violent fluctuations with "others", our discussions are only focusing on road sections and intersections. Although the traffic accidents reduction effects are well functional with both road sections and intersections, the effects with road sections seem more obvious than that with intersections in average.

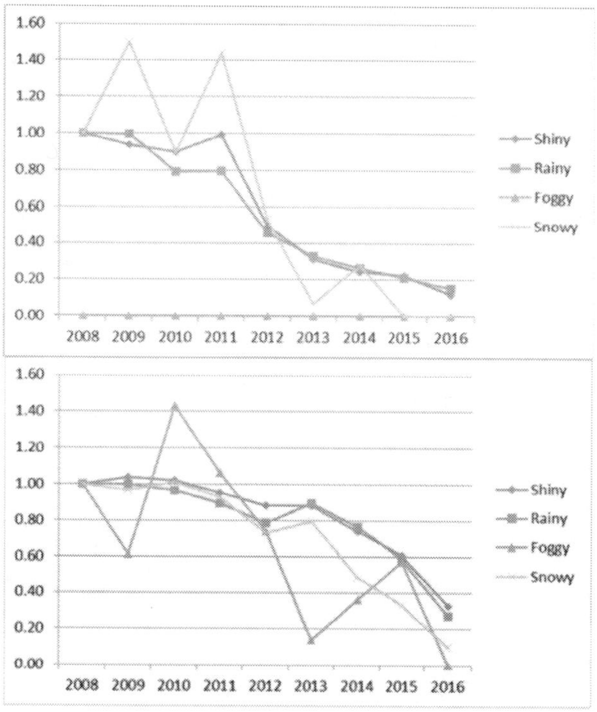

Figure 9. Changes of elderly drivers' accidents over the years in terms of weather, considering a value of 1.00 in 2008 (top: Subaru cars; bottom: other cars)

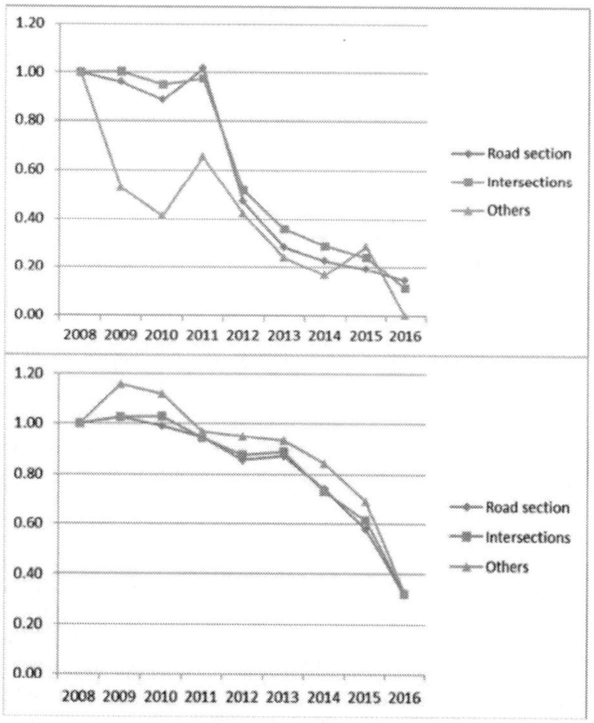

Figure 10. Changes of elderly drivers' accidents over the years based on road environment, consideirng a value of 1.00 in 2008 (top: Subaru cars; bottom: other cars)

C. *Expected Effects in the Coming Years*

If we consider the AEBS is an innovative product, its diffusion process can be discussed using the method proposed by Rogers [19]. As it is shown in Figure 11, the AEBS is getting into the "early majority" period in Japan as the diffusion rate is 16% in 2015 (Figure 1). Then, in the Tenth Fundamental Traffic Safety Program of Japan [20] released by Cabinet Office in 2016, the Japanese government emphasized that it is very important to utilize the innovative technology to reduce the number of fatalities due to traffic accidents. Therefore, it is expected that the number of AEBS users may increase rapidly in the coming years.

As mentioned in Section 1, in Japan, the 24-hour traffic fatalities (dead within 24 hours due to traffic accidents) were 3,904 persons in 2016. The goal set by the government is less than 2,500 per year around by 2020. As one important countermeasure, the AEBS and other ADAS equipment will be functional to ensure the universal mobility and accessibility.

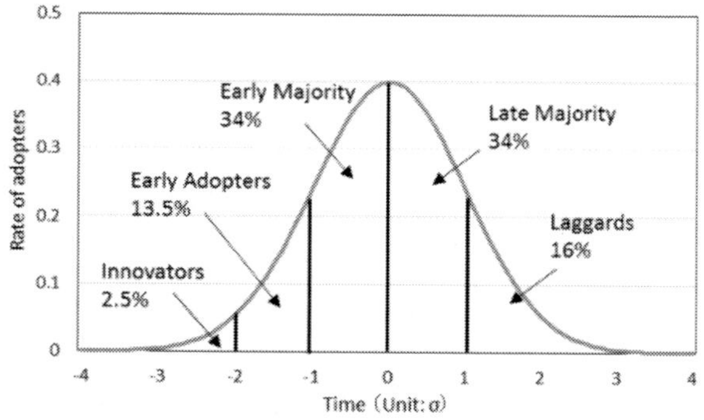

Figure 11. Adopter categories (Source: [19]).

IV. Conclusion and Future Work

In this paper, several comparative analyses on the effects of the ADAS represented by the AEBS equipment are implemented. These analyses revealed an important finding. The ADAS equipment is really effective for the drivers, especially elderly drivers, to reduce traffic accidents. As a result, cars equipped with ADAS equipment might be considered as a smart solution to realize the universal mobility and accessibility of the elderly people in the super-aging society.

As the future work, the following issues will be taken into consideration: 1) the question whether there is an incompatibility with some ADAS equipment, since many different types of equipment are existing in the car market; 2) the question whether drivers should be forced to purchase the ADAS equipment; 3) another similar comparison analysis extended to other countries.

Acknowledements

This study was partly sponsored by a grant (H29) from Japan Safe Driving Center and JSPS KAKENHI Grants Number JP17K06612.

References

[1] Comprehensive Transportation Planning Consortium of Chukyo Metropolitan Area, "Report of the Fifth Person Trip Survey in 2011". [Online]. Available from: *http://www.cbr.mlit.go.jp/kikaku/chukyo-pt/persontrip/p01.html*, last accessed in Jan. 2018.

[2] National Police Agency, "On the Traffic Accidents in 2016". [Online]. Available from: *https://www.npa.go.jp/toukei/koutuu48/H28_setsumeishiryo.pdf*, last accessed in Jan. 2018.

[3] R. Ando, K. Higuchi, and W. Liu, "A Comparative Analysis on Elderly Car Drivers", Presentation at the 15th European Automotive Congress, No. 95, Madrid, Oct. 3rd-5th, 2017.

[4] Y. Nishihori1, J. Yang, R. Ando, and T. Morikawa, "Understanding Social Acceptability for Diffusion of Autonomous Vehicles in Japan Focusing on Drivers", Journal of the Eastern Asia Society for Transportation Studies, in print, 2018.

[5] RnR Market Research, "Research on Global & China Advanced Driver Assist Systems (ADAS) Industry, 2015". Available from: *http://www.rnrmarketresearch.com/research-on-global-china-advanced-driver-assist-systems-adas-industry2015-market-report.html*, last accessed in Mar. 2018.

[6] R. J. Davidse, "Older Drivers And Adas: Which Systems Improve Road Safety?", IATSS Research, Vol.30, Issue 1, pp.6-20. 2006. [Online]. Available from: *https://www.sciencedirect.com/science/article/pii/S0386111214601515*, last accessed in Jan. 2018.

[7] J. C. Winter et al. "Effects of adaptive cruise control and highly automated driving on workload and situation awareness: A review of the empirical evidence", Transportation Research Part F: Traffic Psychology and Behavior, Vol.27, Part B, pp.196-217. DOI: 10.1016/j.trf.2014.06.016.

[8] J. B. Cicchino, "Effectiveness of forward collision warning and autonomous emergency braking systems in reducing front-to-rear crash rates", Accident Analysis & Prevention, Vol.99, Part A, pp.142-152, Feb. 2017. Doi: 10.1016/j.aap.2016.11.009.

[9] J. Son, M. Park, B. B. Park, "The effect of age, gender and roadway environment on the acceptance and effectiveness of Advanced Driver Assistance Systems", Transportation Research Part F, Vol.31, pp.12-24. May 2015. Doi: 10.1016/j.trf.2015.03.009.

[10] F. Biondi, R. Rossi, M. Gastaldi, and C. Mulatti, "Beeping ADAS: Reflexive effect on drivers' behavior", Transportation Research Part F: Traffic Psychology and Behaviour, Vol. 25, Part A, pp. 27-33, July 2014. Doi: 10.1016/j.trf.2014.04.020.

[11] M. Dotzauer, S. R. Caljouw, D. de Waard, and W. H. Brouwer, "Intersection assistance: A safe solution for older drivers?", Accident Analysis & Prevention, Vol. 59, pp.522-528, Oct. 2013. Doi: 10.1016/j.aap.2013.07.024.

[12] J.K. Caird, S.L. Chisholm, and J. Lockhart, "Do in-vehicle advanced signs enhance older and younger drivers' intersection performance? Driving simulation and eye movement results", International Journal of Human-Computer Studies, Vol. 66, Issue 3, pp.132-144, Mar. 2008. Doi: 10.1016/j.ijhcs.2006.07.006.

[13] J. H. Kim, "Effectiveness of Collision Avoidance Technology". [Online]. Available from: *https://www.worksafecenter.com/safety-resources/PDF/Collision_Avoidance_Technology_Report.pdf*, last accessed in Jan. 2018.

[14] Ministry of Land, Infrastructure, Transport and Tourism. [Online]. Available from: *http://www.mlit.go.jp/jidosha/anzen/01asv/resourse/data/H27souchakudaisuu.pdf*, last accessed in Jan. 2018.

[15] TTRI (Toyota Transportation Research Institute), "Research Report 2016-1: Impacts of Automonous Vehicles on Urban Traffic and Transportation (in Japanese)", 2017.

[16] Subaru, [Online] Available from: *https://www.subaru.co.jp/car/special*, last accessed in Jan. 2018.

[17] Japan Automobile Manufacturers Association, Inc. "Active Matrix Database System". [Online]. Available from: *http://jamaserv.jama.or.jp/newdb/eng/index.html*. last accessed in Jan. 2018.

[18] Statistics Bureau, "Survey on the Social Lives in 2011". Ministry of Internal Affairs and Communications. [Online]. Available from: *http://www.stat.go.jp/data/shakai/2011/index.htm*, last accessed in Jan. 2018.

[19] E. M. Rogers, "Diffusion of Innovations," 5th ed. Free Press, New York, 2003.

[20] Cabinet Office, "The tenth fundamental traffic safety program". [Online]. Available from: *http://www8.cao.go.jp/koutu/kihon/keikaku9/english/pdf/part1chapter1_section2.pdf*. last accessed in Jan. 2018.

The Role of the Internet and Technology in the Well-being of People with Physical Disabilities

Alexandra Young, Tom Dening, Chris Greenhalgh
University of Nottingham
Nottingham, UK
Email: Alexandra.young@nottingham.ac.uk; tom.dening@nottingham.ac.uk; chris.greenhalgh@nottingham.ac.uk

Abstract— **Online activity can play an important role in the lifestyle and well-being of people living with physical disabilities. This mixed methods study involving 45 participants from around Nottinghamshire serves to illustrate the multiple roles Information Technology (IT) and the Internet can play in supporting the mental and physical well-being of people with lifetime disabilities. 44 of the 45 participants were active users of IT, to a greater or lesser extent, with uses ranging from vital communication devices, to hobbies and small business use.**

Keywords- Physical Disability; Internet; Information Communication Technologies; ICT; Information Technology; IT; Well-being.

I. Introduction

The Internet and technology play an increasingly important role in the day to day lives of people across the UK. This change certainly includes people living with physical disabilities. The trend continues to increase with a wider range of adaptive and assistive technologies becoming available and affordable, with smartphones becoming almost ubiquitous. As more information from the government and health services is nowadays located online, this is a trend not just built from want, but also from necessity.

The research presented is an exploratory study, looking at how people with physical disabilities are using the Internet on a day to day basis, and the role this has on well-being, rather than focusing on interventions or specific activities. Research in this area is sparse and inconclusive [1][2], with the majority of the literature looking at a specific aspect of Internet use or well-being, such as improvements in the classroom [3], or promotion of physical activity and peer connection through online resources [4], [5]. The literature also supports a similar focus on information sharing and social support, with little insight into how this fits into people's daily Internet activities [6][7][8][9].

The rest of the paper is structured as followed; in section 2 we describe the recruitment and analysis methods used in this study. In section 3 we cover the results of data collection, and discuss the findings of the study, and the limitations of the methods utilized. In section 4 we concluded what impact the Internet had on the physical and mental well-being of participants in this study. Section 5 covers further work, and how the findings of this study have been fed into a wider project on Internet use and well-being.

II. Methods

The data for this study were collected using a mix of face to face interviews, and online questionnaires.

Participants for the interview study were contacted through collaboration with Nottinghamshire County Council. In order to protect the anonymity of potential participants, the Council was supplied with the inclusion criteria (over 18, receiving assistance from the adult social services department for a physical disability, and living in their own home rather than residential care), and asked to send out an information letter inviting people to respond and participate in the study. People receiving these letters were then free to respond, or not, if they were interested in the study. In all, 18 participants were recruited from 150 total responses across phone, email, text and post, with interested parties making contact through email being directed to the questionnaire after the interview study was filled. However, in the end, 16 interviews were completed due to two participants withdrawing. The interviews were semi-structured and lasted between 30 and 120 minutes. The interviews were audio recorded and then transcribed for analysis in NVivo [10][11], first using a grounded theory approach [12], and then thematic analysis based on emergent themes from the first coding, as well as those from the questionnaire data for comparison.

Participants for the online questionnaire were recruited through link sharing on social media (Twitter, Reddit, and Facebook), an advertisement on a participant recruitment website, and word of mouth. Some participants were also directed to the questionnaire after expressing interest in the interview study after it was filled. The questionnaire followed the same outline as the interview script, with a mix of open and closed questions, allowing participants to elaborate on answers or leave comments where appropriate. This allowed the answers to be more directly comparable to those given in the face to face interviews, and create a more useful data source. In total, 29 questionnaires were completed over a two month period. Free text entries in the questionnaire were analysed in a similar way to the questionnaire transcripts in order to create a level of comparison in the emergent themes between the two data sources.

III. Results and Discussion

In total, 45 people participated across the two streams, with 16 participating in interviews and 29 completing the online questionnaire. The participants were from a broad age range, spanning from 18 to 85 across the two groups, and had a variety of different physical disabilities; it is significant to note here that people were not asked what diagnosis or disability they had, and any data on this was disclosed freely either in the interview or using a free text option in the questionnaire. Significantly, the group of participants was made up of a mix of people who had experienced the disability their whole lives, and people who had become disabled later in life, either through an accident or the onset of a related condition. This allowed a greater level of insight into the role the Internet had played during the rehabilitation and adaptation process, and how the use had changed over time. The comparison between people who had always lived with a disability, and those who had come disabled allowed a view into the use of technology and the uptake of and acceptance of it between the two groups.

The data from both groups showed clearly that the Internet and technology play a significant role in the daily activities of the people who took part in this study. This included learning about how to adapt products to suit the individuals' specific needs, and reaching out and finding, or forming peer support groups; of 29 questionnaire participants, 18 used time on the Internet to find peer support groups. Over three quarters of participants used at least one form of social media every day, for a mix of purposes, including peer support and charity information. One participant cited the Internet as "a lifeline" that had allowed them to adapt to their disability, moving from a tool for occasional shopping and emails, to something which has allowed them to adapt existing items in the house for continued use. Another participant had a voice controlled 'possum' unit set up to operate their computer, as well as to control the television, door locks, and phone from their wheelchair in order to retain a greater level of independence during the day between assistant visits. Apart from one participant who did not have access to the Internet, all the participants across the interviews and questionnaire group used the Internet to connect with family and friends, and to continue to access hobbies and support networks, for example through writing, singing groups, online gaming, and social media. Alongside information finding, the accessing of support networks was found to be a key theme, and thus should be considered in routine rehabilitation practice.

As mentioned, only one participant did not use the Internet or any technology, beyond television and radio, and had no interest in doing so for either social or rehabilitation purposes. Otherwise, all participants were active users of different technologies, covering a range of devices from smart phones to multiple desktop computers, or multiple devices in use. However, there is likely to be considerable bias arising from the recruitment of the participants. Questionnaire participants were recruited through social media and sharing in charity forums, and the survey itself was hosted online, requiring a certain level of engagement on the Internet in order to find, or receive, the survey link, and interest in order to complete it. Although interview participants did not need to have online access, the recruitment letter for the interviews specifically asked about Internet use for accessing social services and support, which probably discouraged other people who had limited Internet use. Of the people who received information letters about the study from the County Council, about 100 replied saying that they felt unable to participate in a face-to-face interview because of lack of access to laptops, smartphones and/or the Internet. A further 40 of the responses were from people who used the Internet but felt that they did not use it enough, or to access social services support, and would therefore not be of any help in the study.

IV. Conclusions

Although the number of participants was small across both the questionnaire and interview elements of the study, the nature of the responses indicates that the Internet and communication technologies play a significant role in the ability to adapt existing resources to fit condition specific needs, and in supporting mental well-being of people with physical disabilities. For many of the participants, it allowed a way to connect with peers and expand existing support networks in ways which may not have been possible due to travel accessibility, or indeed geographic distance from peers with a similar condition. It is therefore important to consider the potential positive influence of online sources of support and information, and the roles they can play beyond normal Internet usage for adults living with physical disabilities.

V. Further Work

Building on the findings in this study, further work is planned to understand the impact of Internet use on the well-being and information seeking practices of people diagnosed with early onset dementia, and how this use changes as the condition progresses and changes interactions with technology.

Acknowledgment

The lead author, Alexandra Young, is supported by the Horizon Centre for Doctoral Training at the University of Nottingham (RCUK Grant No. EP/L015463/1) and by Nottinghamshire County Council, the external partner.

REFERENCES

[1] L. P. Cheatham, "Effects of Internet use on well-being among adults with physical disabilities: A review," *Disabil. Rehabil. Assist. Technol.*, vol. 7, no. 3, pp. 181–188, May 2012.

[2] C. Grimaldi and T. Goette, "The Internet and the independence of individuals with disabilities," *Internet Res.*, vol. 9, no. 4, pp. 272–280, Oct. 1999.

[3] C. S. Englert, Y. Zhao, K. Dunsmore, N. Y. Collings, and K. Wolbers, "Scaffolding the Writing of Students with Disabilities through Procedural Facilitation: Using an Internet-Based Technology to Improve Performance," *Learn. Disabil. Q.*, vol. 30, no. 1, pp. 9–29, Feb. 2007.

[4] V. D. Berg *et al.*, "Engagement and satisfaction with an Internet-based physical activity intervention in patients with rheumatoid arthritis," *Rheumatology*, vol. 46, no. 3, pp. 545–552, Mar. 2007.

[5] S. L. Hopps, M. Pépin, and J.-M. Boisvert, "The effectiveness of cognitive-behavioral group therapy for loneliness via inter relaychat among people with physical disabilities.," *Psychother. Theory Res. Pract. Train.*, vol. 40, no. 1–2, pp. 136–147, 2003.

[6] Finn J, "An exploration of helping processes in an online self-help group focusing on issues of disability," *Health Soc. Work*, vol. 24, no. 3, p. 220–231 12p, Aug. 1999.

[7] D. O. Braithwaite, V. R. Waldron, and J. Finn, "Communication of Social Support in Computer-Mediated Groups for People With Disabilities," *Health Commun.*, vol. 11, no. 2, pp. 123–151, Apr. 1999.

[8] H. Liang and Y. Xue, "Online health information use by disabled people: The moderating role of disability," presented at the International Conference on Information Systems (ICIS 2013): Reshaping Society Through Information Systems Design, 2013, vol. 3, pp. 2798–2813.

[9] M.-L. Drainoni *et al.*, "Patterns of internet use by persons with spinal cord injuries and relationship to health-related quality of life," *Arch. Phys. Med. Rehabil.*, vol. 85, no. 11, pp. 1872–1879, Nov. 2004.

[10] P. Bazeley and K. Jackson, *Qualitative Data Analysis with NVivo*. SAGE, 2013.

[11] N. L. Leech and A. J. Onwuegbuzie, "Beyond constant comparison qualitative data analysis: Using NVivo. School Psychology Quarterly," *Am. J. Orthopsychiatry*, pp. 70–84, 2011.

[12] J. M. Corbin and A. Strauss, "Grounded theory research: Procedures, canons, and evaluative criteria," *Qual. Sociol.*, vol. 13, no. 1, pp. 3–21, Mar. 1990.

TELEPROM-G: A Study Evaluating Access and Care Delivery of Telehealth Services among Community-Based Seniors with Depressive Symptoms

Cheryl Forchuk
Lawson Health Research Institute
London, Ontario, Canada
email: cforchuk@uwo.ca

Puneet Seth
InputHealth
Hamilton, Ontario, Canada
email: puneet@inputhealth.com

Akshya Vasudev
Western University
London, Ontario, Canada
email: Akshya.Vasudev@lhsc.on.ca

Amer Burhan
Western University
London, Ontario, Canada
email:
Amer.Burhan@sjhc.london.on.ca

Tony O'Regan
Lawson Health Research Institute
London, Ontario, Canada
email: Tony.oregan@lhsc.on.ca

Abstract— **Depression has been identified as a leading cause of frailty worldwide. Factors which contribute to an effective implementation of Telehealth/eHealth among seniors living with depressive symptoms remain understudied. Research has linked technology-geared mental health care delivery to better healthcare outcomes. Rigorous scientific evidence on the efficacy of ehealth technology, for example smartphone applications, is lacking. The solution tested in this study was a web-based Telemedicine and Client-Reported Outcome Measurement platform, using a Chromebook device. Applying a mixed method design, this pilot study generated valuable insights regarding factors which facilitate positive experiences for seniors participating in an eHealth intervention. Further research studies on the implementation of the platform with seniors appears to be feasible since the present study was able to successfully recruit 30 client participants and retain 87% until the end of study. Results related to participants' perceptions of the smart technology suggest device features need modification to facilitate older adults' comfort with the platform.**

Keywords-depressive symptoms; eHealth; mental health; seniors; technology; Telehealth.

I. INTRODUCTION

Depression is considered the single largest contributor to global disability [1], highly prevalent among older adults, 65 years old and over [2][3], and linked to poor health outcomes, including reduced quality of life, comorbidity, and increased frailty [4]. Studies suggest that health care interventions delivered through Telehealth/eHealth technology may potentially improve health outcomes among seniors with depressive symptoms [5][6], and reduce hospital emergency and rates of admissions among seniors [7].

The improvement of health outcomes attributable to technology-geared mental health care delivery has been inconsistent across studies. Aburizik et al. [8] found that mobile psychotherapy sessions had a non-significant effect on chronic disease self-management and health-related quality of life. Piette et al. [9] found that the use of interactive voice response to maximize mobile health monitoring made no difference in improving health status, medication adherence, and days in bed. Pecina et al. [10], in a web-based intervention study of 205 American patients with comorbid medical and mental health disorders involving depression, found no significant effect on reported physical and mental status. Donker et al. [11], in a recent systematic review of eight smartphone studies for mental health care delivery, found that none demonstrated rigorous scientific evidence on the efficacy of smartphone applications. The scarcity of evidence on the efficacy of eHealth may be partially due to the fact that the majority of research on the use of mobile health technology has solely investigated the pre-implementation phase [12].

The TELEPROM-G pilot-study tested the feasibility for implementation of a Collaborative Health Record (CHR), a web-based platform designed for outcome-based health services delivery.

The rest of this paper is organized as follows. Section II outlines aims of the study. Section III discusses methodology. Results and discussion of results are presented in Section IV and Section V respectively. Section VI provides conclusions from the study and suggestions for future research.

II. AIMS OF THE STUDY

The primary aims of study were to: (1) examine the feasibility of implementing and evaluating the CHR platform in the older adult population; and 2) determine if further modifications to the CHR platform or deployment would be necessary. This study was guided by the following research questions: (1) what is the rate of participant recruitment from outpatient mental health programs? (2) what are the participants' perceptions of the CHR platform? (3) what is the estimated effect size for the impact of the CHR platform on community integration, quality of life, and other health indicators of senior participants?

III. Methodology

A. Participants

Eight Health Care Providers (HCPs) identified thirty of their clients who met the criteria for inclusion into the study: being diagnosed or self-diagnosed with depression, aged 65 years or older, living in the community, and willing to give informed consent to participate. Exclusion criteria consisted of having significant cognitive deficits, as determined by a Mini Mental State Examination (MMSE) [13] score of 19 or less, and scoring less than 5 on the Geriatric Depression Scale (GDS) [14]. A member of the research team recruited client participants who met inclusion criteria by obtaining their voluntary, informed consent.

B. Procedures

The study used a mixed method design to collect quantitative interview data prior to the study's intervention and at six months after the initial interview. This paper reports on quantitative results from individual client interviews. A structured interview was conducted upon enrollment with each participant. At the end of the interview each participant received a Wi-Fi enabled Chromebook device.

Participants were trained on how to use the Chromebook device and the web-based Collaborative Health Record (CHR) created by InputHealth, a Canadian digital health company. The CHR platform allowed for both synchronous and asynchronous communication between patients and care providers. This included receiving and completing questionnaires such as personal health information and self-assessments, a comprehensive mobile client record, and the opportunity for secure HCP-client communication such as face-to-face video sessions (virtual visits).

The research team ensured CHR platform user accounts and passwords were created for both HCP and client participants, that HCP participants were capable of sending invitations for virtual visits, and that all appropriate questionnaires were added to the CHR platform. Likewise, the research team ensured that client participants understood how to complete questionnaires and respond to virtual visit requests.

Quantitative data, consisting of baseline and final interviews, were conducted utilizing eight measures to assess demographics, community integration, depressive symptoms, suicidal ideation, quality of life, physical health, utilization of emergency services, and perceptions of smart technology.

The demographics form that was used covered basic items, such as age, gender, ethno-racial identity, indigenous status, and marital status. It also included questions assessing the presence of chronic physical illnesses and psychiatric illnesses, including symptoms of mental illness, types of psychiatric diagnoses, and total number of psychiatric admissions, as well as age at first contact with the mental health system, and age at first psychiatric admission. A Likert Scale measured participants comfort with various technologies and related tasks (using computers, tablets, smartphones, technology in general, Internet browsing, sending/receiving email, sending/receiving text messages, and using social media, etc.).

Community integration was measured via the Community Integration Questionnaire (CIQ) [15]. The CIQ consists of 15 questions and is intended as a brief, reliable, objective measure of a person's level of integration in the home and community. The overall score can range from 0 to 29, with a higher score indicating better integration. The CIQ can be divided into three subscales corresponding to home integration, social integration, and productivity [16]. The CIQ is based heavily on types of activities (e.g.., shopping, cooking), and assumes independent participation is a sign of greater integration than supported or mutual co-participation.

Depressive symptoms were measured using the short version of the GDS [14][17]. The GDS has been tested and used extensively with the older population in a variety of settings including the community and acute and long-term care settings. The overall score ranges from 0 to 15, with higher scores indicating higher levels of depression. Scores above 8 are indicative of major depression; while anything less indicates subclinical depressive symptoms [14].

The Geriatric Suicide Ideation Scale (GSIS) [18] was used to measure suicide ideation. The GSIS is a 31 question scale with scores ranging from 31 (low/no suicide ideation) to 165 (high level of suicide ideation). Total scores can be divided into 4 subscales: suicide ideation, death ideation, loss of personal and social worth, and perceived meaning in life. The GSIS has shown good internal consistency (total score a = 0.93, subscales a = 0.82 to 0.84) and good construct and criterion validity when measured against other validated instruments for depression, hopelessness, life-satisfaction, and psychological well-being [18].

The Health, Social, Justice Service Use (HSJSU) questionnaire [19] was utilized to assess the number of emergency room visits, phone calls to crisis lines, visits by crisis teams, and ambulance trips made in the preceding six months.

Quality of life was measured via the Quality of Life Brief Version (QoL-BV) [20], [21]. The QoL-BV measures both objective quality of life (i.e., what people do and experience) and subjective quality of life (i.e., what people feel about these experiences). Consisting of 74 items, this tool spans eight domains: living situation, daily activities and functioning, family relations, social relations, finances, work/school, legal/safety issues, and health. Internal consistency for people with mental illness ranges from $\alpha =$ 0.56 to 0.87 [21].

Physical health was measured in the demographics form and by the Short-Form Health Survey (SF-12) [22]. The SF-12 measures health on eight domains: general health, physical functioning, role limitations due to physical health, bodily pain, energy/vitality, social functioning, role limitations due to emotional health, and mental health.

The Perception of Smart Technology Form [23] was used to measure several domains of participants' experience with the CHR platform. These domains include level of helpfulness, ease of use, and clarity, in addition to information on the frequency of CHR platform use and functionality preferences.

IV. Results

Descriptive statistics and mean comparisons using paired sample t-tests were conducted for each of the outcome measures between time-one and two interviews. These comparisons excluded participants who did not complete the measure during time-two.

A. Characteristics of client participants

Participants had a mean age of 72.8 (SD = 4.8) and ranged from 65 to 84 years of age. The sample consisted of 12 (40%) males and 18 (60%) females, all of whom had contact with their family and were unemployed/retired. Education level of the participants varied, with three (10%) participants having completed grade school education, 14 (46.7%) having completed high school education, and 13 (43.3%) having completed post-secondary education. Sixteen (53.3 %) participants indicated that they lived alone, and 14 (46.7%) indicated that they lived with family. The top two psychiatric conditions in the sample were anxiety disorders (n = 17) and mood disorders (n = 27), with 20 (66.7%) participants having two or more psychiatric conditions (Fig 1). Regarding comorbid physical and psychiatric conditions, over 90% of participants had comorbidities, such as arthritis (33.3%), high blood pressure (33.3%), and anxiety disorders (56.7%). All participants were taking medication for their mental illness, and half of the participants stated that they had had a psychiatric hospitalization in their lifetime. At study onset, 2/3 of participants had existing Wi-Fi set up, 12 (40%) participants reported feeling extremely comfortable with technology, whereas no participants reported feeling extremely comfortable with technology at study end.

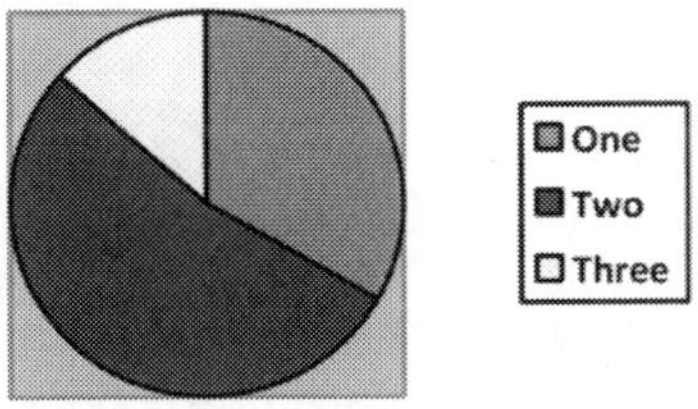

Figure I. Number of psychiatric conditions reported by client participants (N = 30)

B. Retention and attrition rates

Twenty six (87%) of the client participants completed the study. Four (13%) participants withdrew from the study before the second interview; one participant withdrew from the study shortly after enrolment for an unknown reason and three others withdrew later due to health reasons. As such, for time-two interviews there were 12 (46%) male participants and 14 (54%) female participants, with a mean age of 72.85 (SD = 4.46). On the HSJSU questionnaire, all participants who withdrew indicated that they had not talked to a health or social service provider over the phone in the past month. These participants had all experienced side effects from medication, but had not terminated their usage of the medication(s). They also obtained higher mean scores on the SF-12 pain subscale (M = 81.25, SD = 37.5) compared to the other participants (M = 49.04, SD = 31.21) but the difference was not statistically significant (p = 0.071). Overall, these participants did not differ significantly from the other 26 participants on any measures during the interview at time-one.

C. Analysis of outcome measures

This pilot study tested the implementation of CHR platform and recruited 30 client participants. Therefore, statistically significant results of outcomes were not primarily pursued. Paired samples t-tests were utilized to compare CIQ total scores, GDS total scores, and GSIS total scores, and QoL-BV domain scores between time-one and time-two (see Table 1 for total score comparisons). As anticipated, no significant differences were found among any of the subscale domains or total scores of outcome measures between interviews. The mean difference on CIQ was 0.72 (t (17) = 0.80, p = 0.44); GSIS total scores 3.12 (t (24) = 0.67, p = 0.50); GDS total scores 0.33 (t (23) = 0.59, p = 0.56); whereas the mean differences on the QoL-BV domain scores ranged between -396.12 (t (25) = -0.45, p = 0.65) and 0.15 (t (25) = 1.2, p = 0.24). Paired samples t-tests were also employed for the HSJSU. A significant higher proportion of participants reported experiencing prescription medication side effects during interview time-one than interview time-two (t (22) = 2.31, p < 0.05). Finally, physical and mental health information from the eight domains on the SF-12 was compared utilizing paired samples t-tests. The analysis found no significant differences between mean scores on any of these domains between times one and two.

TABLE I. MEAN COMPARISONS FOR OUTCOME MEASURES

Outcome Measure	First Interview n	First Interview Mean (SD)	Second Interview n	Second Intervie w Mean (SD)
Total CIQ scores	23	14.89 (5.47)	23	15.04 (5.26)
Total GDS scores	28	7.93 (3.63)	25	7.72 (3.65)
Total GSIS scores	30	77.97 (21.9)	26	74.04 (22.27)
General Life Satisfacti on score from QoL-BV	30	4.12 (1.06)	26	4.02 (1.17)

D. *Perceptions of smart technology at time-two interview analysis of outcome measures*

The Perception of Smart Technology Form was administered at the final interview to assess client participants' perceptions of the CHR platform, and the Chromebook device. On a scale ranging from one to seven, client participants found the CHR platform helpful [M (SD) = 5.10 (1.61)], enjoyable [M (SD) = 4.67 (1.59)], and fast to use [M (SD) = 4.62 (1.69)] (see Table 2). However, participants had mixed responses in terms of ease of use, with some reporting that the program was relatively easy to use [M (SD) = 4.43 (2.09)] while others rating it lower on simplicity to use [M (SD) = 3.90 (1.73)] (see Table 2). Participants also had mixed responses regarding the reliability of the tablet [M (SD) = 4.29 (1.60)], and regarding whether the tablet and program gave them more or less independence [M (SD) = 3.56 (1.69)] (see Table 3).

TABLE II. PERCEPTIONS OF CHR PLATFORM AT TIME-TWO

Perceptions	n	Mean (SD)	Standard Deviation
Helpfulness	21	5.10	1.61
Enjoyment	21	4.67	1.59
Speed	26	4.62	1.69
Ease of use	21	4.43	2.09
Simplicity	21	3.90	1.73

Responses were given on a 7 point Likert scale, with 1 indicating the most negative response and 7 indicating the most positive response.

On a section of the Perceptions of Smart Technology Form, participants were asked specific questions related to their use of the Chromebook device. In terms of how they felt about connecting with their health care providers, on average, they indicated that they felt mostly satisfied. Participants reported liking the communication abilities, personal usage and accessibility of the tablet. However, participants reported not liking the technical difficulties, small size and potential scams associated with using the tablet. Roughly one-third of participants (n = 9) felt that the tablet and CHR platform had improved their healthcare.

TABLE III. PERCEPTIONS OF CHROMEBOOK DEVICE AT TIME-TWO

Perceptions	n	Mean	Standard Deviation
Helpfulness	25	4.92	1.50
Enjoyment	25	4.84	1.97
Ease of use	25	3.76	2.12
Simplicity	25	3.20	1.94
Reliability	25	4.29	1.60
Independence	25	3.56	1.69

Responses were given on a 7 point Likert scale, with 1 indicating the most negative response and 7 indicating the most positive response.

V. DISCUSSION

The purpose of this pilot study was to examine the feasibility of implementing and evaluating the CHR platform among seniors living with depressive symptoms and to determine possible modifications to the CHR platform, through assessment of client perceptions of smart technology at six months of intervention. Regarding the feasibility of implementing and evaluating the CHR platform in the older adult population, the study was able to recruit 30 client participants; of which, 26 (86.67%) successfully completed the study. Recruiting and retaining such rates of participants until the end of the study indicates that the implementation of CHR platform is feasible among seniors with depressive symptoms. These results, related to recruitment and retention of seniors, contrast with the recruitment difficulties experienced in a RCT pilot study [6], wherein the authors had difficulties recruiting participants aged 60 years and over. The study also evaluated potential modifications to the current CHR platform through feedback provided by the Perceptions of Smart Technology Form. Perceptions of client participants regarding the tablet device were mainly positive. On a scale of one to seven, participants rated the simplicity of the device as 3.20 and helpfulness as 4.92. Viewing the results of technology questions in the Perception of Smart Technology Form and the Demographic Data Form, it is noticeable that scores were mainly positive among seniors who had previous experience of Internet use, higher education, and who were younger in age and living with a relative. Wildenbos et al. [24] found similar results in a study which examined barriers and enablers of the use of Telehealth for seniors. These authors indicated that factors enabling seniors to use technology include higher levels of education, receiving help from others to use the Internet, being aged less than 70 years old, and comfort with using the Internet. An improvement to increase seniors' comfort with the CHR platform might include being able to connect with clients' phones as well as tablets; a process that would require further development to overcome limitations posed by the current system due to its compatibility with only the Chrome browser. Furthermore, increased communication functions might enhance the delivery of mental health services among community-residing seniors, reducing crises and supporting community integration.

Consistent with results from previous studies [9][10], this pilot study found no significant effect on health outcome measures, including community integration, depression, and quality of life, along with social, health and justice service utilization variables. However, the study found significantly higher rates of participants who experienced lower prescription medication side effects during interview time-two than interview time-one.

A. *Limitations*

The study investigated eHealth technology with seniors experiencing depressive symptoms. While the pilot study successfully recruited the target number of client participants and retained 87% until completion of the study, there are a number of limitations. The small sample size may reduce the study power to detect the effect of the intervention on health outcome measures. The fact that the study had no control group and had a limited length of intervention implies that caution should be used in interpreting the results. Therefore, a larger sample size of participants would be needed to determine the long-term implications of using eHealth technology to connect with seniors with depression living in the community.

B. Implications

Results from the TELEPROM-G study have implications for practice and future research. The study demonstrated potential modifications to the current CHR platform through feedback provided through the Perceptions of Smart Technology Form. To this end, senior participants indicated that they are more likely to have positive experience when eHealth devices are perceived as simple and helpful. Furthermore, the study illustrated demographic characteristics to consider for improving the uptake of eHealth among seniors with depressive symptoms. Characteristics such as having a previous experience of Internet use, higher education, being younger in age, and living with a relative were associated with the senior participants' positive perceptions of technology. The pilot study, having successfully recruited 30 client participants, retained 26 of them for a six-month follow-up, deployed the intervention, and finding 2/3 of participants with existing Wi-Fi set up, has demonstrated that future studies with this population are feasible.

VI. CONCLUSION

This pilot study highlighted the benefits of supporting community integration and reducing health crises and needs and now requires further investigation with a full study. Senior clients experiencing depressive symptoms were provided with a Chromebook device and access to the CHR platform, an application that allowed for enhanced communication with their HCP. The study explored the potential outcomes on physical and mental health as well as the participants' perspectives of the CHR platform and the use of a Chromebook device. Although there were no significant changes on a number of physical and mental health outcome measures, the study's findings illustrated that the use of the CHR platform was helpful, enjoyable and relatively easy to use. In addition, significantly fewer clients reported medication side-effects at six month post-baseline. However, clients suggested that the Chromebook was too small and had encountered technical difficulties with it, suggesting that an alternative, perhaps more familiar, piece of equipment such as a phone or desktop computer may be preferable. The implementation of tele-mental health using the CHR platform is feasible as this study was able to recruit 30 older adults and retain 87% until the completion of the study. It is recommended that future studies investigate the use of eHealth technologies with a larger sample of seniors experiencing depressive symptoms and using different platforms and personal electronic devices. A research design that includes a control group, such as a randomized controlled trial, would be ideal in investigating eHealth technologies further.

ACKNOWLEDGMENTS

This research was supported by Canadian Frailty Network, Project File Number: CAT 2015-TG1.

The authors present this paper on behalf of the TELEPROM-G research team: Richard Booth, Keri-Leigh Cassidy, Mary Chambers, Alastair Flint, Boniface Harerimana, Marnin Heisel, Jeffrey Hoch, Wanrudee Isaranuwatchai, Maxine Lewis, Daniel Lizotte, Karl Looper, Fiona Nolan, Casey Oliver, Damon Ramsey, Jeffrey Reiss, Soham Rej, and Abraham Rudnick.

REFERENCES

[1] World Health Organization. Depression and other common mental disorders global health estimate. [Online]. Available from: http://apps.who.int/iris/bitstream/10665/254610/1/WHO-MSD-MER-2017.2-eng.pdf?ua=1/ [Retrieved: January 2018].

[2] Center for Diseases Control. Depression is not a normal part of growing older. [Online]. Available from: https://www.cdc.gov/aging/mentalhealth/depression.htm [Retrieved: January 2018].

[3] D. P. Chapman and G. S. Perry, "Depression as a major component of public health for older adults," Preventing Chronic Disease, Vol. 5 (1), pp.1, Jan. 2008. Available from: https://www.ncbi.nlm.nih.gov/pmc/articles/PMC2248771/pdf/PCD51A22.pdf [Retrieved: January 2018].

[4] C. Buigues, C. Padilla-Sánchez, J. F. Garrido, R. Navarro-Martínez, V. Ruiz-Ros, and O. Cauli, "The relationship between depression and frailty syndrome: A systematic review," Aging and Mental Health, Vol. 19, pp. 762-772, Oct. 2014, doi. 10.1080/13607863.2014.967174.

[5] E. Stanmore, B. Stubbs, D. Vancampfort, E. D. de Bruin, and J. Firth, "The effect of active video games on cognitive functioning in clinical and non-clinical populations: A meta-analysis of randomized controlled trials," Neuroscience and Biobehavioral Reviews, Vol. 78, pp. 34–43, Jul. 2017 doi:10.1016/j.neubiorev.2017.04.011.

[6] K. L. Lichstein, F. Scogin, S. J. Thomas, E. A. DiNapoli, H. R. Dillon, and A. McFadden, "Telehealth cognitive behavior therapy for co-occurring insomnia and depression symptoms in older adults," Journal of Clinical Psychology, Vol. 69, pp. 1056-65, Aug. 2013, doi:10.1002/jclp.22030.

[7] L. Godleski, D. Cervone, D. Vogel, and M. Rooney, "Home telemental health implementation and outcomes using electronic messaging," Journal of Telemedicine and Telecare, Vol. 18, pp. 17-9, Jan. 2012, doi:10.1258/jtt.2011.100919.

[8] A. Aburizik, L. Dindo, P. Kaboli, M. Charlton, K. Dawn, and C. Turvey, "A pilot randomized controlled trial of a depression and disease management program delivered by phone," Journal of Affective Disorders, Vol. 151 (2), pp. 769-774, Nov. 2013, doi:10.1016/j.jad.2013.06.028.

[9] J. D. Piette, J. B. Sussman, P. N. Pfeiffer, M. J. Silveira, S. Singh, and M. S. Lavieri, "Maximizing the value of mobile health monitoring by avoiding redundant patient reports: Prediction of depression-related symptoms and adherence problems in automated health assessment services," Journal of Medical Internet Research, Vol. 15, pp. e118, Jul. 2013, doi:10.2196/jmir.2582.

[10] J. L. Pecina, G. J. Hanson, H. Van Houten, and P. Y. Takahashi, "Impact of telemonitoring on older adults' health-related quality of life: The Tele-ERA study," Quality of Life Research, Vol. 22, pp. 2315-21, Nov.2013, doi: 10.1007/s11136-013-0361-5.

[11] T. Donker, K. Petrie, J. Proudfoot, J. Clarke, M. R. Birch, and H. Christensen, "Smartphones for smarter delivery of mental health programs: A systematic review," Journal of Medical Internet Research, Vol.15 (11), Nov. 2013, doi: 10.2196/jmir.2791.

[12] S. T. Peek, E. J. Wouters, J. van Hoof, K. G. Luijkx, H. R. Boeije, and H. Vrijhoef, "Factors influencing acceptance of technology for aging in place: A systematic review," International Journal of Medical Informatics, Vol. 83 (4), pp. 235-248. Apr. 2014, doi: 10.1016/j.ijmedinf.2014.01.004.

[13] M. F. Folstein, S. E. Folstein, and P. R. McHugh, "Mini-mental state: A practical method for grading the cognitive state of patients for the clinician," Journal of psychiatric research, Vol. 12 (3), pp. 189-198, Nov. 1975, Retrieved 2018-01-30 from: https://www.ncbi.nlm.nih.gov/pubmed/1202204

[14] J. A. Yesavage, et al., "Development and validation of a geriatric depression screening scale: A preliminary report", Journal of Psychiatric Research, Vol.17, pp. 37-49, Dec. 1983, Retrieved 2018-01-26 from: http://www.ncbi.nlm.nih.gov/pubmed/7183759

[15] B. Willer, K. J. Ottenbacher, and M. L. Coad, "The community integration questionnaire: A comparative examination," American Journal of Physical Medicine and Rehabilitation, Vol. 73 (2), pp. 103-111, Apr. 1994, Retrieved 2018-01-26 from: http://www.ncbi.nlm.nih.gov/pubmed/8148099

[16] B. M. Stalnacke, "Post-traumatic stress, depression, and community integration a long time after whiplash injury," Mental Illness, Vol. 2 (1), pp. e4, Apr. 2010, doi: 10.4081/mi.2010.e4.

[17] J. L. Sheikh and J. A. Yesavage, "Geriatric Depression Scale (GDS): Recent development of a shorter version", in Clinical Gerontology: A guide to assessment and intervention, New York, NY: The Haworth Press, pp.165-173, 1986.

[18] M. J. Heisel and G. L. Flett, "The development and initial validation of the Geriatric Suicide Ideation Scale," American Journal of Geriatric Psychiatry, Vol. 14 (9), pp. 742-751, Sept. 2006, doi: 10.1097/01.JGP.0000218699.27899.f9.

[19] P. Goering et al, "The at home/chez soi trial protocol: A pragmatic, multi-site, randomised controlled trial of a Housing First intervention for homeless individuals with mental illness in five Canadian cities," British Medical Journal Open, Vol. 1, pp. e000323, Jan. 2011, doi:10.1136/bmjopen-2011-000323.

[20] A. Lehman, "A quality of life interview for the chronically mentally ill," Evaluation and Program Planning, Vol. 111, pp. 51-62, Dec 1988, doi.10.1016/0149-7189(88)90033-X

[21] A. Lehman, E. Kernan, and L. Postrado, Toolkit for evaluating quality of life for persons with severe mental illness [Online] Available from: https://www.hsri.org/publication/toolkit_evaluating_quality_of_life_for_persons_with_severe_mental_illn [Retrieved: January 2018].

[22] J. Ware, M. Kosinski, and S. D. Keller, "A 12-Item Short-Form Health Survey: Construction of scales and preliminary tests of reliability and validity," Medical Care, Vol. 34 (3), pp. 220-33, Mar. 1996, Retrieved 2018-01-30 from: http://www.ncbi.nlm.nih.gov/pubmed/8628042

[23] C. Forchuk, et al. "Mental health engagement network: An analysis of outcomes following a mobile and web-based intervention," Journal of Technologies in Society, Vol. 11 (2), pp. 1-10, Jun. 2015, Retrieved 2018-01-30 from: http://www.ijt.cgpublisher.com/product/pub.297/prod.16

[24] G. A. Wildenbos, L. Peute, and M. Jaspers, "Facilitators and barriers of electronic health record patient portal adoption by older adults: A literature study," Studies in Health Technology Informatics Vol. 235, pp. 308-312, 2017, doi: 10.3233/978-1-61499-753-5-308.

SAMIoT – Middleware based on IoT for Irrigation Planning on Large-scale Crops

Jose Luis Rivas Viedman, Juliana Sánchez Benítez, Javier Alí Carbonell Gonzáles, Edgar Hincapié
Department of Information Technology and Networks
Colombian Sugarcane Research Center (CENICAÑA)
Cali, Colombia
email: {jlrivas, jsanchez, jacarbonell, ehincapie}@cenicana.org

Armando Ordóñez
Intelligent Management Systems
University Foundation of Popayan
Popayán, Colombia
email: jaordonez@unicauca.edu.co

Hugo Ordoñez
Faculty of Systems Engineering
University of San Buenaventura Cali
Cali, Colombia
email: haordonez@usbcali.edu.co

Abstract— **Monitoring of large-scale crops may require Wireless Sensor Networks to collect information in real time. These networks require the integration of diverse devices and sensors. Middlewares have been used to facilitate the integration of heterogeneous applications and services. This article presents SAMIoT, a middleware aimed at improving the production of sugarcane through the optimization of water use. The middleware monitors the matric potential of the soil to determine the right moment to irrigate. A solution based on the proposed middleware was developed for the sugarcane crops in the Cauca River Valley in Colombia.**

Keywords-middleware; Internet of Things (IoT); Wireless Sensor Networks (WSNs); matric potential; efficient irrigation.

I. Introduction

Large-scale farming can be extended on large expanses of land. Monitoring these crops may require the deployment of Wireless Sensor Networks (WSN) based on the Internet of Things (IoT). These networks interconnect a large number of sensors to collect data from the crops in real time [1]. Obtaining an increasing amount of information from the plants enables farmers to make quick and accurate decisions.

In the sugar crops, some variables, such as the electrical resistance [2], the capacity of water absorption and the degree or thermal level of the soil are continuously monitored. These variables are used to calculate the matric potential or volumetric water content of the soil. The matric potential allows determining the most appropriate moment for irrigation. Through this process, an efficient use of the water can be achieved, with the consequent impact on the environment and the profitability of farmers.

Various methods have been proposed for the irrigation planning. Some methods are based on the quantification of components of the water balance. This quantification allows estimating a permissible level of water exhaustion in the soil. Other methods are based on monitoring the water of the soil or plants [3].

Cenicaña is a Colombian entity dedicated to the research of sugarcane. Cenicaña has tested and recommended other methods for the irrigation planning such as the use of the Cenirrometer tank [4], the installation of groundwater observation wells, and the verification of soil humidity [5].

The water balance is the most used method among cane growers in the Cauca River valley. This method requires incorporating aspects related to the hydrophysical properties of soils. However, in the Cauca River valley, there is a high heterogeneity of soils (about 238 soil varieties) and a high variability of precipitation. This variability makes it necessary to have humidity and granular matrix sensors to continuously monitor the energetic state of the water in the soil, thus improving the accuracy of irrigation planning.

These methods allow to trigger alarms according to the amount of water available for the plant [6] or with an optimum soil humidity (i.e., between ± -20 and ± -80 kilopascals (KPa)) [7].

To achieve an efficient use of water, it is necessary to determine the consumption and availability of water required for crops. IoT offers an alternative to automate and optimize data capture.

WSNs are used in agriculture to address different problems. Most of these networks use a single system or application or are deployed only in a particular area of interest [8].

The sensors used in agriculture are not endowed with processing. The middleware presented here is called SAMIoT and allows communication between these sensors within a WSN [9]. These nodes are connected to Smart Agricultural Nodes in an IoT environment. This network can handle near real-time events, through TCP (Transmission Control Protocol) sockets supported by the modular extension of Node.js [10].

SAMIoT allows the integration of elements to facilitate the configuration of a device in the IoT ecosystem. The system enables users to manage and configure new conditions, send commands to the node, collect information from the sensors connected to this node, and send data to a server. The middleware includes notification services that inform if the values received from the sensor exceed a predefined min-max threshold value.

The middleware was applied to monitor variables that contribute to reducing the uncertainty that exists in the irrigation planning. Due to resource constraints of the project, the middleware described here is validated in a crop with six nodes; however it is designed and is envisaged to be used in large-scale crops.

The rest of this paper is organized as follows. Section 2 presents the related work. Section 3 describes the architecture of the middleware. Section 4 details the implementation of the prototype and Section 5 concludes.

II. RELATED WORK

Some tools can be found on the market for IoT development, such as ReMMoC (A Reflective Middleware to Support Mobile Client Interoperability) [11], OpenIoT (Open source blueprint for large scale self-organizing cloud environments for IoT applications) [12] and WebNMS [13]. Most of these tools focus on solutions for general use in homes and urban areas, leaving aside the restrictions or limitations of the agricultural environment. Some have focused on providing interoperability and reconfiguration to mobile applications [14]. Other works present architectures for the deployment of services in a semantic environment [15] like LinkSmart (formerly known as HYDRA). This latter approach allows the creation of ambient intelligence (AmI) applications, through the combination of service-oriented architecture (SOA) and an architecture based on semantic models.

ReM-MoC [11] is a reflective middleware platform that dynamically adapts its link and protocol to allow interoperability with heterogeneous services. Also, the ReMMoC programming model is integrated into the platform. This model is based on the concept of Web Services of abstract services for the development of mobile applications through a middleware platform.

Recently there has been a need to give users control over the IoT. This requirement increases the importance of middleware since it simplifies the development of new services and technologies or integrates them with existing ones. Hence, the importance of projects like OpenIoT [12] (FP7-287305) that develop a middleware platform allowing the configuration of utility-based applications, as well as cloud-based detection services.

Platforms such as WebNMS [13] seek to help companies achieve their IoT / M2M (Machine to Machine) objectives. WebNMS allows making timely decisions and optimizing processes. WebNMS supports customization and extensibility between domains. Despite its advantages, this tool is aimed at professionals with high knowledge in software development.

Regarding agriculture, few studies can be found that show the development of middlewares to support a large number of sensors. In [14], it is shown the digitization of some aspects of agriculture such as agricultural production, livestock, aquatic products and forestry industry through Information Technology, Internet connectivity, and the IoT. Also, in the field of agriculture, it is widespread to find applications dedicated to the monitoring of the environment in various disciplines, such as, control of livestock sheds, and precision agriculture.

On the other hand, CarrIoTs [16] presents a cloud-based platform service for IoT projects. This platform supports M2M communications and focuses on scalability at the network level. CarrIoTs does not guarantee storage security and offers limited interoperability. Table I shows the gaps between five alternatives to develop IoT solutions.

TABLE I. RELATED WORKS (GAPS)

	Service Discovery	Cloud deployments	On-premises deployments	Unlimited heterogeneous frames /sensors	Open source
ReMMoC	✓		✓		✓
WebNMS		✓			
OpenIoT	✓	✓	✓	-	✓
Carriots	✓	✓			
Hydra / LinkSmart	✓	✓			✓

Most of them are based on services discovery, which limits the support to multiple frames or custom frames. On the other hand, some limitations do not allow implementation on various servers.

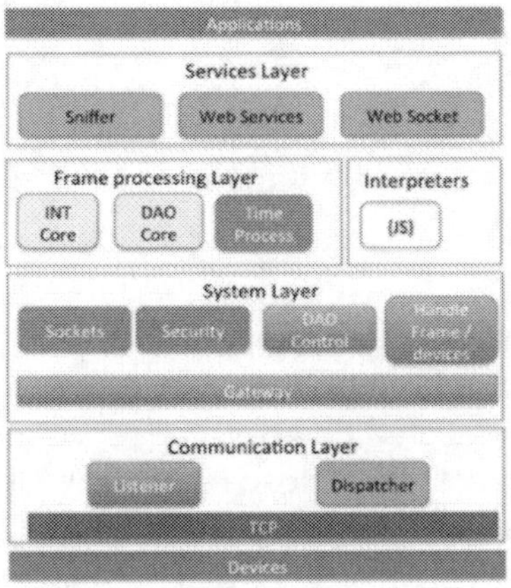

Figure 1. Middleware architecture.

III. ARCHITECTURE OF THE MIDDLEWARE

The architecture components are described below (see Fig 1).

A. Architecture

the proposed middleware is based on two architectural approaches for middlewares design [17]:

Message-Oriented Middlewares (MOM): here the communication is based on messages that include extra metadata. Compared to event-oriented middlewares, messages are bearers of sender and receiver addresses. In MOM, the listening engine of the proposed middleware receives and processes packets whose frame structure and sender information have been previously defined at the database level.

Middleware based on agents: Since the Internet does not have a single solution for all domains this approach aims at providing some features such as resource management, reduction of network load, code management, asynchronous and autonomous execution, availability, robustness, fault tolerance and adaptability. In this approach, applications are divided into modular programs called agents, to facilitate the injection of events and their distribution through the network, facilitating the design of decentralized systems. In this middleware, agents are represented on a logical layer based on interpreters. This representation makes it possible to offer a fully configurable and extensible middleware solution for the IoT. This solution is also adaptable to different operating environments, and frames.

B. Design

Fig. 2 shows a general abstraction of the architecture showing the communication dependencies between components. The four layers of the architecture are described below:

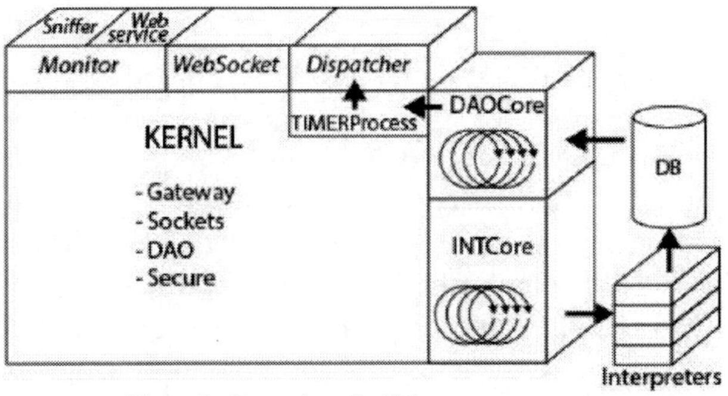

Figure 2. Abstraction of middleware components

1) Communications layer: This is responsible for establishing, controlling, maintaining communication to and from the devices. The *Listener* process has a permanent listening port, while the *Dispatcher* is responsible for sending the commands defined by the users or applications to the *Smart Agricultural Nodes*. These commands can be sent through a console or can be retrieved from commands stored in the database.

2) System layer: This layer is responsible for providing technical and logical interoperability between the smart agricultural node and the middleware. According to ETSI (European Telecommunications Standards Institute), technical interoperability allows linking hardware, software, systems and platforms components to establish a machine-to-machine communication. This layer focuses on the communication protocols and the necessary infrastructure so that they can interoperate. This layer also provides the objects that will be instantiated in each interpreter. Besides, this layer also carries out the frame and checksum validation, manages the DAO (Data access Object) layer and various interpreters.
At the security level, there are two primary processes. Firstly, the MOM is used to send the sender's IP address as well as the serial number or identification registered in the database in the extra data. In this way, only the connection between a node and the middleware is allowed. Secondly, once the connection is established, and the frame is received, this frame is sent to a security process that verifies if the type of incoming frame has been previously registered in the database. Once a satisfactory response is obtained, the quality of the data is validated with the value of the checksum of the frame. On the other hand, the security of the transmission is left to the TCP / IP protocol.

3) Frame Processing layer: This layer is made up of three processes

DAOCore: This layer is based on the DAO pattern that makes the logic of the middleware independent of the persistence, reduces the transaction complexity and improves the performance of container-managed transactions. This pattern enables interpreters to interact with different databases. The middleware for the information capture requires a minimum structure at the database level. In addition to storing data from the collected variables, this database stores several types of valid frames (table 2). Likewise, the names, IP or MAC addresses of the Smart Agricultural Nodes, devices or datalogger are stored to comply with the MOM approach. Finally, the topic identifiers for each WebSocket are also stored.

INTCore: This process manages the interpreters. These interpreters process and parse the diverse message formats (frames). These frames are received from the clients and defined in the database.

TIMERProcess: This process is permanently monitoring the rules in the database. When a condition is met, this is processed and dispatched to the smart Agricultural Node through the command dispatcher. This sending can be done to retrieve lost data due to connection failures, or to activate actuator devices (open or close the water valves, turn a water pumping on or off).

4) Services Layer: This layer is composed of the following elements:

WebSockets: provides a bi-directional channel of real-time communications for advanced web services and applications. Here, the information from each socket/thread is exposed as a topic and may be consumed by different clients. This method provides a near real-time communication.

Sniffer: This component exposes some events that are occurring within the kernel. Fundamentally it is a TCP service that allows a connection through a Telnet client.

WebServices: Exposes an API to query information or trigger core events. The exposed services are:

- list: list the connected devices.
- Broadcast: Send a message to all connected devices.
- closeByIp: close the connection with a device using the IP address.
- close: Close all client connections.
- closeAll: Close all client connections and restart the core server.
- ReloadInterpreters: restart the interpreter driver and set a newly created interpreter in the middleware.
- sendByIp: Send commands to the Smart Agricultural Nodes.

5) Interpreters

These are routines in JavaScript that process each frame format in a customized way. These methods create instances of the CORE processes, are autonomous and preventive, and translate the frames sent from the INTCore. The user of the middleware can modify two classes. The first to perform the parsing of the frame and to process the information (apply equations, correct data, etc.). The second class is used to adjust the fields to the model before inserting the information into the database.

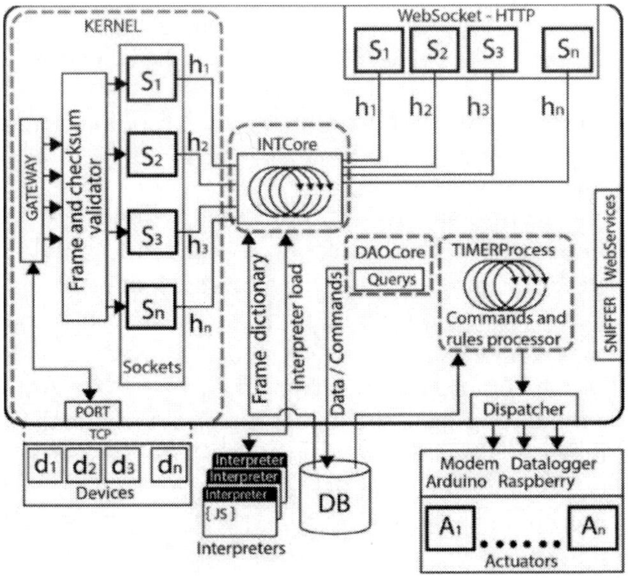

Figure 3. Operation flow of middleware.

Fig. 3 shows the communication diagram of the components. The middleware is listening permanently for a specific port. The clients or devices (dn) are connected to the server using this port via TCP/IP. A TCP socket (sn) is created per client. Each socket is handled by a thread (hn), thus, simultaneous communications with multiple devices are supported.

The information that circulates in each thread is passed to the interpreter, which parses the data according to the pre-established information for each type of device. Thus, a level of security is generated to the frames, since the frames not defined in the database are discarded. On the other hand, the probability of critical neck in the communication flow or an overload is very low because this process is managed by the event loop of Node.js, this method is based on [18]. Once the frame is validated and processed, the data is exposed through a WebSocket service thus offering near real-time communication. Simultaneously the information is sent to the database for storage.

To be accepted, the messages must be identified by a unique type of message according to the frame format defined by the user. Table 2 presents examples of messages received before being processed by interpreters where:

TABLE II. FRAME FORMATS SUPPORTED BY THE MIDDLEWARE

Id	Type	Format
101	Meteorological	101,81508,2017-02-28,14:11:00,26.83,"2017-02-28 14:10:20",26.85,27,"2017-02-28 14:10:10",0.34,52.68,"2017-02-28 14:10:50",53.13,53.56,"2017-02-28 14:10:20",1.15,"2017-02-28 14:10:00",0,0.031,1.144,0.853,0.931,36.02,14.38,1.09 8,"2017-02-28 14:10:20",52.24,"2017-02-28 14:10:20",0,0.014,1.196,0.931,35.94, C508^M
160		160, PL20,2017-02-26,12:30:00,0.00, f948
160	XBee Pluviometers	~�8ï¿½�ï¿½�@Ö¼Rï¿½ï¿½ï¿½|SETI160,PL0006, 2017-02-26,12:30:00,0.00,f944
166	Granular Matrix	166,81506,2017-02-20,09:34:00,23.47,"2017-02-2009:34:00",23.47,23.47,"2017-02-20 09:34:00",0,71.62,"2017-02-20 09:34:00",72.1,72.91,"2017-02-20,09:34:00",1.02,"2017-02-20 09:34:00",0,0.001,1.171,0.061,0,D971

a. Id 101 is a message containing daily readings from different meteorological station sensors. MOM versatility allows the middleware to process the 36 parameters included in this type of frame through the interpreters.

b. The first id 160 corresponds to rainfall variables sent by a device through a GSM (Global System for Mobile communications) network. The message identifier (frame) 160 can be observed.

c. The second id 160, shows a frame that also contains daily readings of rain gauge variables sent through an XBee network. Parameters 1 and 2 are discarded and represent the header of a Xbee frame and its delimiter. Parameter 3 is the identifier of the frame type. Parameter 4 is the name or id assigned to a sensor (rain gauge). Parameters 5, 6 correspond to date and time of the data read by the sensor. Finally, there is the checksum parameter, which represents the sum of the number of bytes of parameters 3 and 4; in other words, 9 + N bytes (See Table III).

d. Id 166 corresponds to a frame that contains readings of granular matrix sensors. With this data, the matric potential or volumetric content of soil water is calculated.

TABLE III. FRAME FORMAT IN XBEE NETWORK.

Order	Parameter		
	Name	# Bytes	Hexadecimal representation
1	XBee Heading		
2	Delimiter		
3	Frame type	3	31 36 30
4	Sensor ID	6	50 4c 30 30 30 36
5	Reading	N	XX XX XX
6	Checksum	1	XX

The middleware also validates the quality of the frame through the checksum processing. This task is performed by the interpreter, the quality of the data is validated by the user by adding or subtracting the checksum parameters.

IV. IMPLEMENTATION

A case study was carried out on the irrigation planning in a large-scale sugarcane crop. The system processes requests and frames with measurements of water conditions in the soil. With these variables, the soil matric potential (PMS from its Spanish initials) is calculated. PSM indicates the total amount of water available to be absorbed by the plant. In this scenario, the behavior of water in the soil of a sugarcane crop is evaluated.

The crop has loamy soil, is located at 1200 meters above sea level, having the coordinates 3.4281 (latitude) and -76.3071 (longitude). The frames with the information are sent through a hybrid network that combines the DigiMesh topology (ZigBee network) and a point-to-point network (Mobile Cellular Network) (see Fig. 4). This configuration was selected due to project constraints in spite of the fact that the middleware has a sequence of TCP sockets.

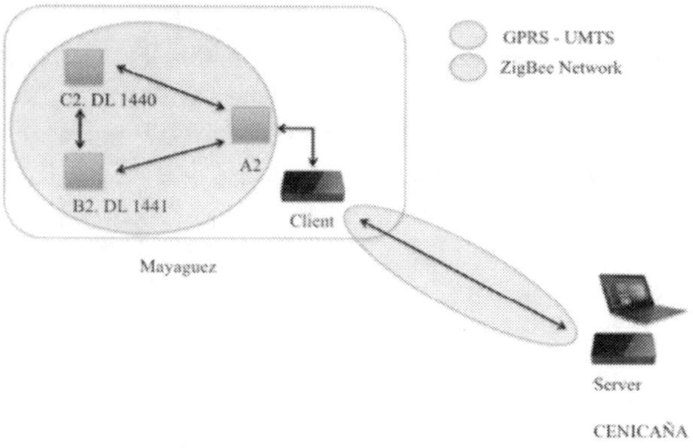

Figure 4. Hybrid network implemented in the monitoring site [47]

Fig. 4 shows the union of two topologies and their point of convergence as follows.

In this topology, the nodes are connected as a mesh network. The second topology (highlighted in blue) supports a client/server model. In the latter, the client modem is connected in series with the XBee® modules and the server modem to the remote computer terminal in CENICAÑA. To communicate the server modem and the client, these devices must be located in an area covered by a mobile cellular telephone network. To configure the network, all devices (XBee® modules, dataloggers, and modems) share a common language (protocol). XBee® modules are assembled on serial cards and provide a serial interface. These modules are connected to the data loggers and the modem through its RS 232 serial port.

TABLE IV. DEPTH AND GROUPING OF GRANULAR MATRIX SENSORS

Sensor MG	Group	Depth
1, 2, 3	P1	30 cms
4, 5, 6	P2	45 cms

Table IV presents the granular matrix sensors and the depth in which they were deployed.

Fig. 5 shows the behavior of the matric potential for each sensor of a granular matrix of the Smart Agricultural Node. This node receives data from six sensors separated into two groups P1 and P2 (at a depth of 30 cm and 45 cm from the soil surface respectively). The sensors are located in a soil with physical characteristics similar to the most of the plants in the crop. The data is sent to the middleware with a format type 166 (table III) at 15-minute intervals. An average of these variables is calculated by the interpreter, according to the frame type. Also, the calibration equation (1) is applied to each reading of each sensor for the calculation of the matric potential [19]. This equation describes the relationships between the resistance in kilo-ohms ($k\Omega$) of the sensors and the soil water potential in kilopascals (kPa). Next, the variables involved in calculating the matric potential are described:

$$PM = \frac{4.093+(3.212*R)}{1-(0.009733*R)-(0.01205*T)} \qquad (1)$$

where PM is the potential of the soil matric in kPa, R is the sensor reading in $k\Omega$, and T is the estimated or measured soil temperature in °C.

The values of matric potential resulting from the application of the calibration equation allow defining mainly two levels of interest to program irrigation works. When the values are lower than -80 kPa, the plants begin to have difficulty extracting water from the soil, and there is a high probability that the crop will suffer from water stress. Conversely, values above 0 KPa, the soil is considered near the saturation point, as shown in Fig. 6.

As the tension increases, the availability of water is lower. In contrast, as the tension decreases, the availability of water is higher, this relationship is known as "change of soil water potential." The available water is between ± -20 kPa and ± -80 kPa; according to criteria established in Cenicaña through experimentation with weighing lysimeters or soil containers described in [20].

Based on these maximum and minimum values, a series of notifications are implemented in the middleware. These messages include push notifications or emails to inform the people in charge of irrigation. The deployment zones of the sensors have approximately a variability of 8 ° C in the soil temperature. Thus, the ranges between ± -20 and ± -80 kPa compensate this temperature difference in the range of 17 and 25 ° C [48].

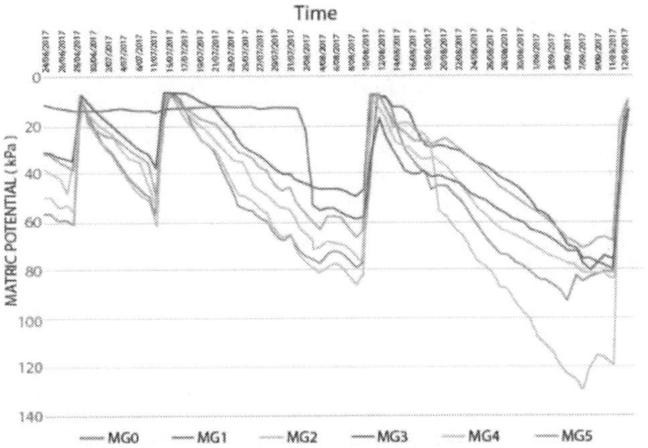

Figure 5. Soil matric potential by sensor

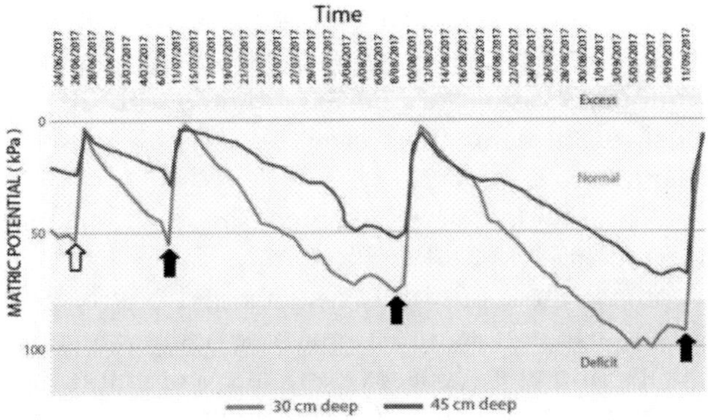

Figure 6. Matric potential vs. time.

Fig. 6 shows curves of average matric potential. It can be seen that on 06/26/2017, just before the irrigation scheduled for 11/07/2017, there was a precipitation event according to rainfall data from the Cenicaña weather station. This rainfall caused an increase in soil humidity (the average matric potential was -53 kPa at a depth of 45 cm, and -24 kPa at 30 cm depth). This situation did not allow observing the change of soil humidity and the behavior of the regular drainage period.

On 08/08/2017 the irrigation began at the "appropriate" moment when the water content of the soil reached a limit close to the deficit. The irrigation scheduled for 11/09/2017 started when the volumetric water content of the soil was in deficit conditions (it can be seen the drainage before irrigation and the recharge period after irrigation). Also, this graph allows visualizing the curve of the readings of sensors at a depth of 30 cm. It can be seen that the decrease in water humidity is faster on the surface due to the heat of the ambient temperature.

In general, the volumetric water content of the soil is very close to the established limits. Water and nutrients remain within the area of highest absorption. Thus, the values stayed close to the field capacity.

With the information of the water content of the soil, people in charge of irrigation planning can make better decisions. Irrigation is carried out only when the soil humidity is at an appropriate level (when), and it can be known when to stop (how much).

V. Conclusions and Future Work

This paper presented the design and implementation of an IoT middleware for the irrigation planning in crops of large expanses of land.

The middleware is composed of four main modules: The CORE allows associating hardware components, software, systems and platforms to establish a machine-to-machine communication. This module focuses on the communication protocols and the subjacent infrastructure. The DAOCore module frees the logic of the middleware (business) from persistence, reducing the complexity of transactions. The INTCore module manages the interpreters that process and parses the messages (frames) received from clients. Finally, the Monitor module sends the commands defined by the users or applications to the Smart Agricultural Nodes. This module generates a bidirectional real-time communication channel for advanced web services and applications and exposes the events that are occurring within the core.

An IoT solution was developed based on the proposed middleware. This solution aims at capturing data from granular matrix sensors, processing this data and calculating the matric potential. This potential allows making decisions on irrigation planning (when and how much).

As future work, it is planned to generate an interpreter automatically when a frame type is defined. Also, the middleware is expected to be used to monitor the matric potential of the soil in the Cauca River Valley. Thus, apart from generating a solution for irrigation, it is expected to be able to acquire a broad knowledge about the behavior of the matric potential in different types of soil and microclimates. This information can be used to analyze other crops and support other widely accepted irrigation models such as the water balance. Finally, a performance evaluation of the multithread processing and communication is envisaged.

References

[1] T. Liu, Y. W. Guan, Y. Q. Yan, L. Liu, and Q. C. Deng, "A WSN-Oriented Key Agreement Protocol in Internet of Things," Appl. Mech. Mater., vol. 401, pp. 1792–1795, 2013.

[2] C. C. Shock, J. M. Barnum, and M. Seddigh, "Calibration of Watermark Soil Moisture Sensors for Irrigation Management," Int. Irrig. Show, February 1998, pp. 139–146.

[3] F. R. Lamm, J. E. Ayars and F. S. Nakayama, "Microirrigation for Crop Production - Design, Operation, and Management," vol. 13, Elsevier, 2006.

[4] J. R. Cruz and T. S. Jorge, "El Cenirrómetro: Un Programador Visual de Riegos,(in English: El Cenirrinometer: a visual planner of risks)" Proc. IV Cong. Colombiano de la Asociación de Técnicos de la Caña de Azúcar, Sept.1997, pp. 207-2016.

[5] J. Torres, J. Cruz, and F. Villegas, "Avances técnicos para la programación y el manejo del riego en caña de azúcar (in English: Technical developments in the planning and management of sugar cane irrigation)". Segunda ed. Serie técnica No. 33. Cali. CENICAÑA, 2004.

[6] L. Zotarelli, M. D. Dukes, and K. T. Morgan, "Interpretación del Contenido de la Humedad del Suelo para Determinar Capacidad de Campo y Evitar Riego Excesivo en Suelos Arenosos Utilizando Sensores de Humedad (in English: Understanding of the soil moisture to determine the capacity soil and avoid excesive irrigation in sandy soils through moisture sensors)". The Institute of Food and Agricultural Sciences (IFAS), pp. 2–5, 2013.

[7] A. C. McCarthy, N. H. Hancock, and S. R. Raine, "Development and simulation of sensor-based irrigation control strategies for cotton using the VARIwise simulation framework," Comput. Electron. Agric., vol. 101, pp. 148–162, 2014.

[8] T. Ojha, S. Misra, and N. S. Raghuwanshi, "Sensing-cloud: Leveraging the benefits for agricultural applications," Comput. Electron. Agric., vol. 135, pp. 96–107, 2017.

[9] J. Haule, M. Kisangiri, "Deployment of Wireless Sensor Networks (WSN) in Automated Irrigation Management and Scheduling Systems: a review," Proc. Science, Computing and Telecommunications (PACT), 2014 Pan African Conference, July 2014, pp. 86–91. doi:

10.1109/SCAT.2014.7055144

[10] A. Ojamaa and K. Duuna, "Assessing the security of Node.js platform," Proc. *7th Int. Conf. Internet Technol. Secur. Trans.* , 2012, pp. 348–355.

[11] P. Grace, G. S. Blair, and S. Samuel, "ReMMoC: A Reflective Middleware to Support Mobile Client Interoperability," OTM Confederated International Conferences" On the Move to Meaningful Internet Systems," 2003, pp. 1–18.

[12] OpenIoT Consortium, "Open source solution for the internet of things into the cloud," January 2012, http://www.openiot.eu [Accessed on: 2018-02-23].

[13] Web NMS, "WebNMS Framework" [Online]. Available: https://www.webnms.com/webnms/. [Accessed on: 2018-02-23].

[14] D. Yan-E, "Design of intelligent agriculture management information system based on IoT," Proc. - 4th Int. Conf. Intell. Comput. Technol. Autom. ICICTA 2011, vol. 1, March 2011, pp. 1045–1049, doi: 10.1109/ICICTA.2011.262.

[15] W. Zhang and K. M. Hansen, "Semantic web based self-management for a pervasive service middleware," Proc. 2nd IEEE Int. Conf. Self-Adaptive Self-Organizing Syst. SASO, Oct. 2008, pp. 245–254, doi: 10.1109/SASO.2008.14.

[16] Altair, "Carriots a platform as a Service (PaaS) for the development of IoT and M2M projects", [Online]. Available: https://www.carriots.com/que-es-carriots. [Accessed on: 2018-02-23].

[17] M. A. Razzaque, M. Milojevic-Jevric, A. Palade, and S. Cla, "Middleware for internet of things: A survey," IEEE Internet Things J., vol. 3, no. 1, pp. 70–95, 2016.

[18] B. Tomáš and K. Žáková, "Node.js based remote control of thermo-optical plant," Proc. 12th Int. Conf. Int. Remote Eng. Virtual Instrum., Feb. 2015, pp. 209-213, doi: 10.1109/REV.2015.7087293

[19] E. P. Eldredge, C. C. Shock, and T. D. Stieber, "Calibration of granular matrix sensors for irrigation management," Agron. J., vol. 85, no. 6, pp. 1228–1232, 1993.

[20] D. Bahia et al., "Design, installation and calibration of a weighing lysimeter for crop evapotranspiration studies," vol. 2, no. 2, pp. 77–85, 2013.

Experimental Study on Riding Skill for Using Standing Type Vehicles

Differences between Unskilled and Skilled Subjects to Complete Task

Naohisa Hashimoto,
Kohji Tomita, Simon Thompson, Yusuke Takinami
Osamu Matsumoto
Robot Innovation Research Center,
National Institute of Advanced Industrial Science and Technology (AIST)
Tsukuba, Japan.
e-mail: {naohisa-hashimoto, k.tomita, simon.thompson, y-takinami, o.matsumoto}@aist.go.jp

Jyeon Kim
The Department of Control and Information Systems Engineering
National Institute of Technology, Tsuruoka College
Tsuruoka, Japan.
e-mail: jykim@tsuruoka-nct.ac.jp

***Abstract*—Many researchers have attempted to solve existing traffic problems. One potential solution to these problems is to reduce traffic volumes in urban areas. In order for this to happen, a modal shift from conventional passenger vehicles to public transportation and eco-vehicles, including personal vehicles, should be considered. There are several types of personal vehicles; in this study, we focus on standing type personal vehicles for solving last mile/first mile problem. As opposed to bicycles, few people have experience in using standing type vehicles; the skill of riding these vehicles depends on the individual. By understanding the differences between skilled riders and unskilled riders, we would like to study for educational programs or assistant system for riding standing type vehicles. The objective of this study was to analyze the differences between skilled and unskilled subjects riding standing type vehicles. The experiment was performed to gather riding data for comparing the difference. We employed two standing type vehicles for the experiments. One is small, and the other is large. In the experiments, two types of subjects traveled the same course, and yaw, pitch, and roll data, and x-, y-, and z-acceleration data of each subject was gathered as riding data. In addition, time duration to finish the goal was evaluated. From the gathered results, the time duration was considered in this paper. In particular, by using the t-value, it was found that there was a significant difference in the time duration between skilled subjects and unskilled subjects when using a large type standing type vehicle. Thus, if we analyze the skill level for using standing type vehicles, we should consider the time duration to complete a slalom course.**

Keywords - Personal mobility vehicles; Experimental analysis; Standing type vehicles.

I. INTRODUCTION

Increasing urban traffic leads an increase in traffic jams, traffic accidents, and air pollution, all of which have a negative impact on the quality of life [1]-[8]. One possible solution to these problems is to reduce traffic volumes in urban areas. Modal shifts from conventional vehicles to public transportation and eco-vehicles, including personal mobility vehicles, should be considered to reduce urban traffic volumes [9]-[15]. In this study, we focused on personal mobility vehicles to reduce traffic volumes.

Automobiles are the traditional optimal means of transportation as they permit door-to-door transportation. However, in order to address the traffic problems mentioned above, we have to shift at least some movement of people from individual automobiles to public transportation. To resolve this problem, useful and eco-friendly alternative transportation must be provided. Considering the use of public transportation, the first and last mile problem remains, especially for elderly people [9]-[12].

With respect to the key solution of the first and last mile problem, not only personal mobility but also automated vehicles and electric commuter vehicles were proposed by several researchers and projects [11]. It is difficult to solve the problem by only one transportation method as every place has different conditions, laws, users and environment, and user's preferences are different.

In this paper, personal mobility vehicles (vehicles for individual use), are investigated as one of the most effective options for solving the first and last mile problem [12][13][15]. Several other types of individual vehicles are also expected to be used as personal mobility vehicles, such as electric scooters, new one-seater vehicles, and wheelchair-type mobility devices. Standing type personal mobility is the target of this study. In Japan, the use of standing type vehicles on public road is prohibited. As to the acceptance, Pham studied the occupied spaces for standing type personal mobility [16]. As for safety, Lavallee reported an analysis of existing safety regulations for Segways, the legal framework for using these vehicles, and traffic rules [17]. The Australian Capital Territory reported experimental results of acceptance, safety, and effect on the community and the pros and cons of using Segways in community areas [18]. In addition, research on an assistance system for standing type vehicles has been conducted by several researchers [19]-[26], but the statistical data on riding new types of self-balancing vehicles with real subjects and on public roads is insufficient.

As opposed to bicycles, few people have experience in using standing type vehicles; thus, the skill of riding these vehicles depends on the individual. By understanding the differences between skilled riders and unskilled riders, we would like to study for educational programs or assistant system for riding standing type vehicles.

The objective of this study is to analyze the differences between skilled and unskilled subjects riding a standing type vehicle in a preliminary experiment. Before this study, we performed preliminary experiments with only a few subjects under simple conditions [27]. Hence, it was difficult to analyze that data in order to evaluating standing type vehicles. In this study, more experiments were performed to obtain riding data. In the experiment, both skilled and unskilled subjects traveled on the same course, and the yaw, pitch, and roll data, and x-, y-, and z-acceleration data of each subject were obtained as riding data. By comparing the data from two kinds of subjects, the statistical differences were found. These differences are useful for evaluation of the skill of riding standing type vehicles.

The rest of the paper is structured as follows. In Section 2, we present test vehicles. In Section 3, the performed experiments are described. Finally, we conclude the work in Section 4.

II. Test Vehicles

Two types of personal mobility vehicles were used in the evaluation, and they are discussed in detail in this section.

A. Segway

The Segway [15], developed by the Segway Corporation, was employed as a personal mobility vehicle (as shown in Fig. 1). The "Segway® PT i2" model, produced by the Segway Japan Corporation, was employed in this experiment. Segways are currently used in Japan in national parks for conducting tours, on golf courses for player assistance, and zoos, stations, airports, to name but a few of the places, by information service staff and security staff. The security staff at the Tsukuba Designated Zone use Segways in order to improve the efficiency of their patrolling. In addition, some cities and universities in Japan have introduced pilot programs using Segways for multiple purposes. Thus, the Segway is attracting attention as a new type of transportation, enabling personal mobility.

Figure 1. Segway.

B. AIST -Personal Mobility (AIST-PM)

The AIST-PM, which was developed by AIST, is a human-riding wheeled inverted pendulum vehicle [24][27], as shown in Fig. 2.

The features of the AIST-PM are as follows:

1. Smaller and lighter than a Segway
2. Has a suspension system
3. Easily lifted
4. The occupied space is almost equal to the space that one person occupies while walking
5. Maximum velocity is low, and kilometers-per-charge is low, but the total efficiency is good as one-person transportation.

The AIST-PM has two individual controllable wheels in the body, and the stick-shaped handles are attached vertically on each side of the body. Two motors and a computer are installed in the body, and the upper face of the vehicle is the platform on which the subject stands.

The left and right wheels are each driven by direct-current motors (DC-motors), which are controlled by an on-board computer installed in the vehicle. The angles of the wheels are measured by counting the number of encoder pulses, and the angle and angular velocity of the pitch direction of the vehicle are measured using gyro-sensors and an accelerometer. A force sensor attached to the platform of the vehicle detects whether the subject is on or off. Table I shows the specification of AIST-PM.

TABLE I. Specification of AIST-PM[24]

Length, Width	0.43[m], 0.55[m]
Tire diameter	0.13 [m]
Weight	12.6 [kg]
Payload (including a passenger)	80 [kg]
Distance (mile per charge)	About 10 [km]
Height of rider's platform	0.19 [m]
Length of sticks	1.25 [m]
Battery	Lithium-polymer

Figure 2. AIST-PM

III. Experiments

This section discusses the mobile-sensor system used in the experiments, experimental conditions, routes and the results obtained.

A. Mobile Sensor System for Obtaining Riding Data

It was difficult to obtain data from a Segway, so it was therefore easier to use an add-on system which could be used on all of the standing type vehicles tested. An add-on mobile-sensor system was thus manufactured. This system consisted of a laptop computer, a gyro-sensor, a G-sensor, a Global Positioning System (GPS) receiver, and a lithium-ion battery. The configuration of the mobile system is shown in Fig. 3. Figure 4 shows the coordinate system used. By using this system, the following riding data was gathered:

1. Velocity
2. Trajectory
3. Roll, Yaw and Pitch rates
4. x-, y- and z-accelerations
5. Time duration to complete the course, which is estimated by using X, Y, Z and Roll, Yaw, and Pitch rate.

All data were saved at 10 Hz on the laptop computer.

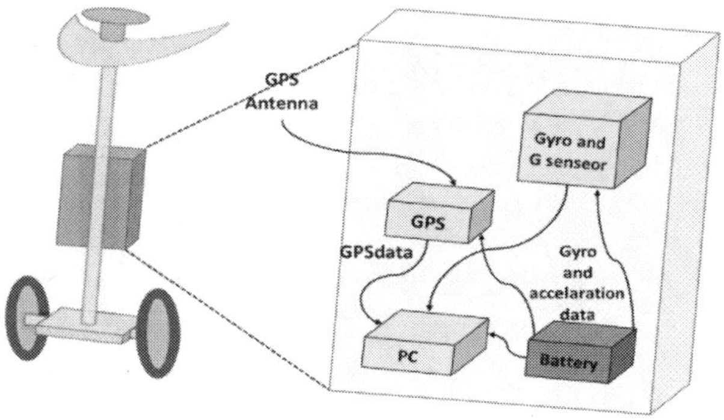

Figure 3. System Configuration

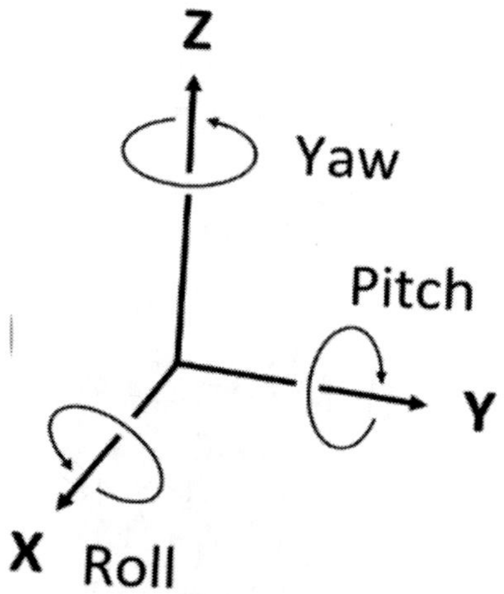

Figure 4. Coordinate system of the sensor

B. Experimental Conditions

We used two kinds of subjects for this experiment, one skilled and the other unskilled. A skilled person is defined in this study as a person who has ridden a standing type vehicle more than 50 times. 28 subjects (15 men and 13 women) were employed for the experiments. The average age of subjects was 41.3. We employed between- subjects approach.

For safety reasons, test subjects wore helmets. The routes were clear of people, and the experiments were conducted only in no rain conditions. In addition, two staff members accompanied the subjects in case of accidents.

C. Experimental Routes

Experimental routes, prepared for this study by AIST, are shown in Fig. 5 and Fig. 6. These routes were designed by AIST by referring the standard course for wheelchair. These routes were planned for only this study and were not associate with any company. The reason why we used two different routes was to consider the size of each vehicle. The subjects were tasked to traverse the experimental routes. The experimental routes included the following tasks:

1). Slalom
2). Going up and down a slope
3). Traveling on a step

The numbers in Fig. 5 and Fig. 6 identify each of the above tasks.

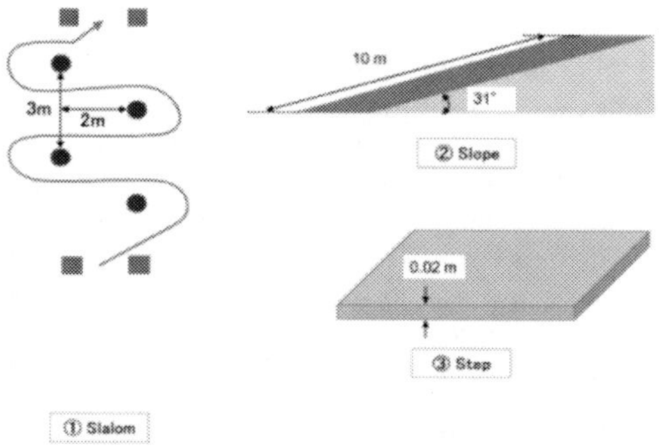

Figure 5. Experimental routes for Segway

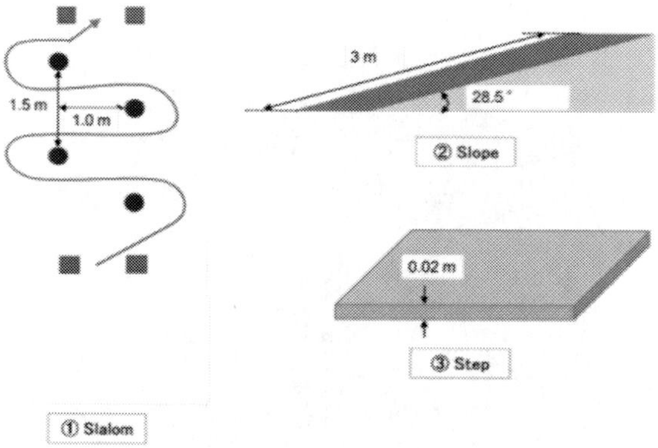

Figure 6. Experimental routes for AIST-PM

D. *Experimental Result*

The experiments were performed. Figure 7 shows the scenes of experiments by using Segway for each task. Figure 8 shows the scenes of experiments by using AIST-PM for each task. By using X, Y, Z accelerations and Yaw, Pitch and Roll rate information, the time was estimated with high accuracy.

Figure 7. Experimental scens by using Segway (From the top: the subject is traveling on slalom, on Slope and on Step)

Table 2 shows the average time duration to complete slalom course by using Segway and AIST-PM. The number of skilled subjects was 3 and of unskilled subjects 25 was respectively. The statistical differences between data sets were evaluated by employing Welch's t-test [28]-[30]. It was found that there was a 5 % statistical difference between the skilled subjects and the unskilled subjects by using Segway on Slalom, shown in Table 3. It is presumed that the skilled subjects could control Segway smoothly and correctly. In addition, they could avoid wasting time by using the ideal trajectory. Hence, skilled subjects followed the unideal trajectory by doing overturning and short turning. By analyzing the trajectory from GPS, the unskilled subjects did not choose the short distance course, but the longer course. Table 4 shows the average time duration to complete slope course by using Segway and AIST-PM. This result has same tendency as the slalom.

On the other hand, it was not found that there was a 5 % statistical difference between the skilled subjects and the unskilled subjects by using AIST-PM on Slalom, shown in Table 3. And it was not found that there was a 5 % statistical difference between the skilled subjects and the unskilled subjects by using AIST-PM on Slope, shown in Table 5. It means that there was less statistical difference between by using the experimental results.

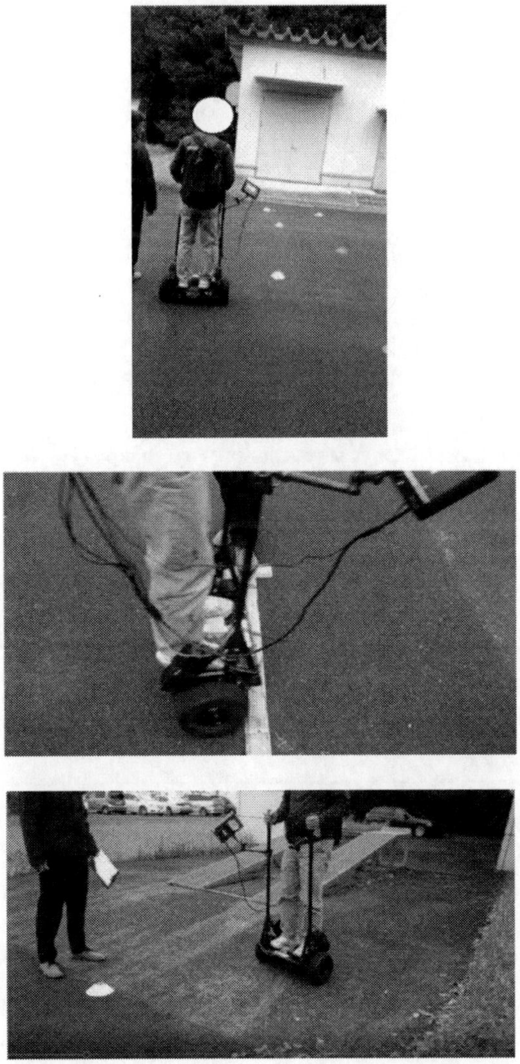

Figure 8. Experimental scens by using AIST-PM (From the top: the subject is traveling on Slalom, on Slope and on Step)

It is presumed that to use AIST-PM is easier than Segway and subjects could get accustomed to the AIST-PM during the lecture period. In addition, the averages between skilled subjects and unskilled subjects are different, but the variance by using AIST-PM is large. Thus, calculated t-value is not enough, and we cannot conclude its difference only from the results. We need to do the experiments more.

As to the step, it was not found that statistical differences between skilled subjects and unskilled subjects about the time to complete.

TABLE II. EXPERIMENTAL RESULTS FOR TIME DURATION ON SLALOM COURSE ON EACH VEHICLE TYPE

	Skilled Subjects	Unskilled Subjects
Segway	13.0 [s]	29.9 [s]
AIST-PM	24.0 [s]	35.5 [s]

TABLE III. EXPERIMENTAL RESULTS FOR T-VALUE OF TIME DURATION ON SLALOM COURSE ON EACH VEHICLE TYPE

	t-value	Degree of Freedom
Between Skilled Subjects and Unskilled Subjects on Using AIST-PM	1.6	25
Between Skilled Subjects and Unskilled Subjects on Using Segway	1.39	26

TABLE IV. EXPERIMENTAL RESULTS FOR TIME DURATION ON SLOPE COURSE ON EACH VEHICLE TYPE

	Skilled Subjects	Unskilled Subjects
Segway	35.2 [s]	49.6 [s]
AIST-PM	21.2 [s]	33.5 [s]

TABLE V. EXPERIMENTAL RESULTS FOR T-VALUE OF TIME DURATION ON SLOPE COURSE ON EACH VEHICLE TYPE

	t-value	Degrees of Freedom
Between Skilled Subjects and Unskilled Subjects on Using AIST-PM	2.067	24
Between Skilled Subjects and Unskilled Subjects on Using Segway	1.39	25

IV. CONCLUSIONS

In this paper, the differences in riding between skilled and unskilled subjects were analyzed for standing type personal vehicles. The standing type vehicles used, and the experiments including the experimental conditions, routes, mobile sensor system, and results were explained in detail. The experiments were performed to gather riding data from skilled and unskilled subjects. In the experiments, both skilled and unskilled subjects traveled the same routes, and the yaw, pitch and roll data, and X-, Y- and Z-acceleration data of each subject was gathered.

By comparing the data from the two kinds of subjects, the time duration was considered in this paper. In particular, by using the t-value, it was found that there was a significant difference in the time duration between skilled subjects and unskilled subjects when using a large type standing type vehicle. Thus, if we analyze the skill level for using standing type vehicles, we should consider the time duration to complete a slalom course. In addition, the importance of the design for standing type vehicles is to consider the friendly or functional interface for traveling on slalom course easily.

We have a plan to analyze the experimental results in different views, including features of subjects and do the experiments with more subjects.

ACKNOWLEDGMENT

This work was supported by JSPS KAKENHI Grant Number 16K18057

REFERENCES

[1] U.S. Department of Transportation, "Beyond Traffic –trends and choices-", 2015.

[2] European Commission website, "https://ec.europa.eu/transport/themes_en", accessed at March 5th, 2018.

[3] K. Doi, T. Hasegawa, S. Kobyashi, I. Sugiyama, and M.Mizohata, "A Study on Quality of Mobility Demanded in Super-aged Cities", IATSS Review, Vol.35, No.3, 2011, pp.182-193.

[4] European Commission website, "http://ec.europa.eu/eurostat/documents/3217494/6856423/KS-05-14-073-EN-N/, accessed at March 5th, 2018.

[5] M. Li, J. Hallam, L. Pryor, S. Chan, and K. Chong, "A cooperative intelligent system for urban traffic problems", Proceedings of the 1996 IEEE International Symposium on Intelligent Control, 1996.

[6] M. Seredynski, and F. Viti, "A survey of cooperative ITS for next generation public transport systems", Proceedings of 19th International Conference on Intelligent Transportation Systems, 2016, pp.1229-1234.

[7] S. Tsugawa, "Promotion of Energy ITS", 2008 EU-Japan Cooperation Forum on ICT Research, 2008.

[8] S. Shladover, "Challenges to evaluation of CO2 impacts of intelligent transportation systems", Proceedings of 2011 IEEE Integrated and Sustainable Transportation System, 2011, pp.189-194.

[9] B. Balcik, B. M.Beamon, and K. Smilowitz, "Last Mile Distribution in Humanitarian Relief," Journal of Intelligent Transportation Systems, Vol. 12, No.2, 2008, pp.51–63.

[10] Mineta Transportation Institute, "Using Bicycles for the First and Last Mile of a Commute", Report No.S-09-02, 2009.

[11] European Commission Report, "Design features for support programs for investments in last-mile infrastructure", 2016

[12] B. Polina, G. Gabriela, and M. J.Luis, "From the Last Mile to the Last 800-ft: Key Factors in Urban Pick-up/Delivery of Goods", Proceedings of 96rd Transportation Research Board, 2017.

[13] Je-Dok Kim, Ho-Jin Lee, and In-Soo Suh, "Strategic Planning on Electric PMV for Sustainable Mobility", Proceedings of 93rd Transportation Research Board, 2014.

[14] V. Renaudin, A. Dommes, and M. GuilbotEngineering, "Human, and Legal Challenges of Navigation Systems for Personal Mobility", IEEE Transactions on Intelligent Transportation Systems, Vol.18, No.1, 2017, pp.171-194.

[15] A. Kornhauser, S. Vin, S. McDonald, N. Serulle, and S. Young, "Deliberations Public Transportation and Shared Mobility", Proceedings of 93rd Transportation Research Board, 2014

[16] T. Pham, C. Nakagawa, A. Shintani, and T. Ito, "Evaluation of the Effects of a Personal Mobility Vehicle on Multiple Pedestrians Using Personal Space", IEEE Transaction of IEEE Intelligent Transportation Systems, 2015.

[17] P. Lavallee, "Pilot project for evaluating motorized personal transportation devices: Segways and electric scooters," Technical report on Centre for Electric Vehicle Experimentation in Quebec, 2004.

[18] "Segway review report: A review of Segway use in the Australian Capital Territory" ACT Government, Justice and Community Safety Tech. Rep., 2012.

[19] M. Ciężkowski, and E. Pawłuszewicz, "Determination of interactions between two-wheeled self-balancing vehicle and its rider", Proceedings of 20th International Conference on Methods and Models in Automation and Robotics, 2015, pp.851-855.

[20] A. Smirnov, A. Kashevnik, I. Lashkov, N. Hashimoto, and A. Boyali, "Smartphone-Based Two-Wheeled Self-Balancing Vehicles Rider Assistant", Proceedings of FRUCT 17, 2015

[21] M. Alqudah, M. Abdelfattah, I. Boiko, and K. Alhammadi, "Dynamic modeling and control design for a self-balancing two-wheel chair", 2016 5th International Conference on Electronic Devices, Systems and Applications, 2016, pp.1-4.

[22] Winglet, http://www.toyota.co.jp/jpn/tech/personal_mobility/winglet.html, accessed at March 5th, 2018.(in Japanese)

[23] R. Ando, and A. Li, "An Analysis on Users' Evaluation for Self-balancing Two-wheeled Personal Mobility Vehicles", Proceedings of 15th International Conference on Intelligent Transpiration Systems, 2012, pp.1525-1530.

[24] N. Hashimoto, Y. Takinami, and O. Matsumoto, "An Experimental Study on Vehicle Behavior to Wheel Chairs and Standing-type Vehicles at Intersection", 13th International Conference on ITS telecommunications, Tampere, Finland, Dec 2013.

[25] Tsukuba Designated Zone Council, http://www.rt-tsukuba.jp/council/ (in Japanese), accessed at March 5th, 2018

[26] ITF Research Reports, "Cycling, Health and Safety", 2013.

[27] N. Hashimoto, J. Kim, K. Tomita, S. Thompson, Y. Takinami, and O.Matsumoto, "Preliminary experiments for evaluation of standing-type personal vehicles", Proceedings of ITS World Congress 2017, Montreal, Canada, Oct 2017.

[28] SPSS Amos, https://www.ibm.com/us-en/marketplace/structural-equation-modeling-sem, accessed at March 5th, 2018.

[29] B. L.Welch, "The generalization of "Student's" problem when several different population variances are involved". Biometrika 34 (1–2): 28–35. doi:10.1093/biomet/34.1-2.28. MR 19277, (1947).

[30] L. Zhiying, and Y. Le, "A segmentation method for crossing ambiguity string based on mutual information and t-test difference", Proceedings of Information, Computing and Telecommunication, 2009.

Towards Smart Public Transport Data

A Specific Process to Generate Datasets Containing Public Transport Accessibility Information

Paloma Cáceres, Almudena Sierra-Alonso, Belén Vela, José María Cavero, Carlos E. Cuesta
Escuela Técnica Superior de Ingeniería Informática
Universidad Rey Juan Carlos, URJC
Móstoles (Madrid), Spain
e-mail: {paloma.caceres,almudena.sierra,belen.vela,josemaria.cavero,carlos.cuesta}@urjc.es

Abstract—**If I was a mother of twins, could I find a route to enable me to get around with my twin baby stroller using public transport? In spite of the relevance of mobility in Smart Cities, there are not many websites or apps with which to generate public transport routes for people with special needs. Of those that do exist, Google Maps is a relevant tool that is employed to calculate routes and find points of interest, while Google Transit Feed Specification (GTFS) is a format used to specify public transport data that allows public transport agents to provide a "feed" complying with this specification. GTFS is employed by Google to calculate a route and represent it on Maps. However, Google Maps does not provide detailed information regarding specific facilities such as accessibility to transit, and GTFS does not specify the structure required to provide that public transport accessibility information. Worse still, it is not easy to find specific and detailed accessibility information that can be downloaded and processed so as to develop services for users. In this work, we propose a systematic method with which to provide accessible public transport datasets in order to improve mobility in Smart Cities. The steps in the process include the extraction of data from the Internet to the generation of open and linked datasets. Moreover, we show a case study in which both datasets for users with special needs and an app prototype that uses those datasets to generate accessible subway routes are developed.**

Keywords-Public transport; accessibility; smart city; open datasets; linked data.

I. INTRODUCTION

Smart cities now appear to be ready to meet the challenge of a more inclusive society that offers the same opportunities for all, and several projects and initiatives have been set up. For example, the Global Initiative for Inclusive Information and Communication Technologies (G3ICT) [1] works to introduce "Smart Cities Programs to Improve Human Rights, Civic Engagement, and Business Outcomes". Another example is World ENABLED (WENABLED) [2], which promotes more inclusive societies working on policies and programs related to human and civil rights. G3ICT and WENABLED are working together on a global strategy for digital inclusion and have identified barriers to smart city accessibility and defined the priority steps required to increase accessibility. One of these steps is "Using open and accessible datasets that include information by and about persons with disabilities" [3]. Smart cities take into account aspects as relevant as, for example education, healthcare, and transportation.

With regard to transportation, we feel that it is necessary to express public transport accessibility and special needs information in a more detailed manner, taking into account that this information is extremely important for a more inclusive society. As we have said, Google Maps is an important tool to calculate routes. To show routes on the map, Google takes data specified in GTFS format. Google Transit Feed Specification (GTFS) [4] defines a "feed": a set of files that describe data concerning public transport. Transport agencies can provide their transport data by means this "feed". Finally, Google employs the "feeds" to calculate the routes and represents them on Maps.

But Google Maps does not provide detailed information about specific facilities such as accessibility to transit, and GTFS does not specify the structure required to provide that public transport accessibility information. In addition, it is not easy to find specific and detailed accessibility information that can be downloaded and processed.

In this work, we propose a systematic method to publish such public transport accessibility data. This method has been validated against real data for the subway in the city of Madrid, Spain (Metro Madrid [5]): we had to validate the generation of accessible subway routes from these data; to do this, we have developed an algorithm which has been implemented as part of the Android prototype app. This prototype (hence the algorithm) makes it possible to obtain an accessible subway route according the Metro Madrid user's needs, a facility that this company does not provide.

The paper is structured as follows: Section 2 presents the state of the art of this work. Section 3 describes our CoMobility and Access@City projects, which are the context of this work. Section 4 introduces some examples of the current state of special needs and accessibility information. Section 5 describes both our proposal, specifying the process used to obtain public transport accessibility datasets, and a case study. Our conclusions and future work are presented in Section 6.

II. RELATED WORKS

To the best of our knowledge, currently there are no projects which fully define accessibility limitations and their relationship to the features of public transport.

However, there exist several semantic models which represent specific aspects of the public transport domain. In some cases, they also include accessible wayfinding information or/and accessibility features, or elements for people with special needs or disabilities. Next, we introduce some the more representative among them.

NaPTAN [6] is a vocabulary with which to identify, in a unique manner, the national public transport access nodes of the United Kingdom. It does not incorporate any aspect of accessibility. The ofi-ontology [7], meanwhile, makes it possible to represent whether a place is accessible to people with mobility problems by means of classes such as AccessFacilities and properties such as is_wheelchair_accessible, but it does not take into account other necessary elements in order to provide blind or deaf people with information. DBpedia [8] has a property denominated as isHandicappedAccessible to indicate whether or not a transit station is accessible. Tube Facility ontology [9] incorporates only step free and lift facilities as accessibility elements (mobility disabilities). Accessibility Ontology [10] is similarly also focused on concepts related to supporting only mobility disability problems. TRANSIT [10] is a specific ontology for transit but it does not incorporate any aspects of accessibility to human transport. Landmark Ontology for Hiking [12] is focused on older adults and allows them to walk less through the use of wheelchairs. It formally represents landmarks for hiking. The European OASIS (Open architecture for Accessible Services Integration and Standardisation) project [13] does not incorporate relevant concepts for needs regarding accessibility to public transport.

Transmodel [14] is a European Reference Data Model for Public Transport Information, which provides both a model of public transport concepts and data structures that may be useful when building information systems related to the different kinds of public transport. It does not, however, provide any information about accessibility. IFOPT metamodel [15] was conceived as an extension of Transmodel. It is a prCEN ("Comité Européen de Normalisation –CEN-" in French) Technical Specification and defines a model (and also the identification principles) for the main fixed objects related to public access to Public Transport (e.g. stop points, stop areas, stations, connection links, entrances, etc.). It already includes specific structures with which to describe accessibility data concerning the equipment of vehicles, stops and access areas.

III. THE CONTEXT: COMOBILITY AND ACCESS@CITY PROJECTS

This work is being developed in the context of two related research projects: CoMobility and Access@City.

CoMobility [16] defines a multimodal architecture based on linked open data for sustainable mobility. Its main goals are to improve citizens' mobility, optimize their trips by combining public transport and the sharing of private transport (e.g., car sharing), and also provide a means for accessible trips.

Access@City [17] is a coordinated project that defines a technological framework in which to process, manage and use open data concerning public transport with the goal of promoting its accessibility. One of its subprojects is Multiply@City [18], which is focused on processing and harmonizing public transport accessibility data in a semantic manner, taking into account that data is provided by different sources and will have different formats. It is, therefore, necessary to integrate accessibility data, obtained from open data and by means of Web scraping, and accessible routes, obtained by employing crowdsourcing techniques with those users who use mobile technologies. Figure 1 provides a general depiction of this project.

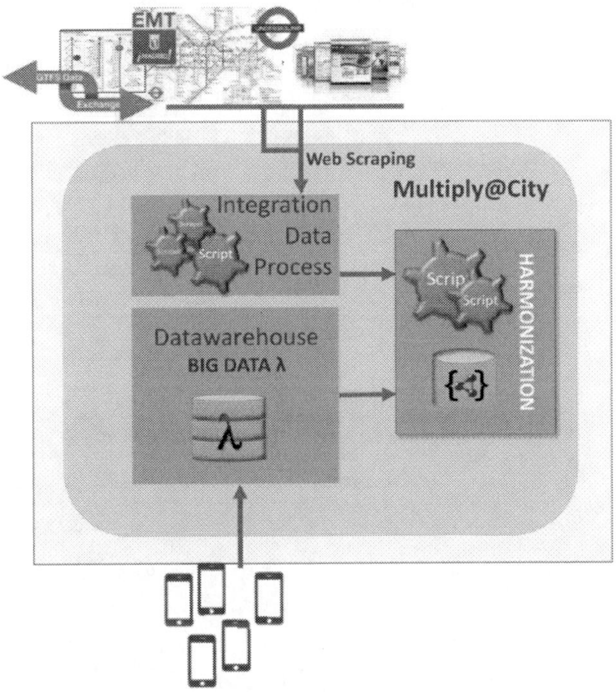

Figure 1 Multiply@City project architecture.

The Regional Consortium for Public Transport in Madrid (CRTM) [19], the Madrid public bus company (EMT Madrid) [20], and the Spanish National Society for the Blind (ONCE) [21] have expressed an interest in the results of our CoMobility and Access@City projects.

IV. The Current State

It is not currently easy for users with special needs to find detailed information regarding public transport on the Internet. In some cases, no accessibility information exists, while in others, it is available only in HTML format (a non-computable format). Only in exceptional cases is it possible to find this information in a computable format.

In this section, we show some examples of how detailed, open and linked the information for users with special needs is. First, we present a study concerning the accessibility information regarding the metro transport media of fourteen European cities. We then go on to describe the GTFS format, which provides the detailed structure employed to specify public transportation schedules and associated geographic information. This can be computable, but has great limitations in terms of specifying transport media accessibility information.

A. Accessibility information of European metro

We have carried out a study on the accessibility of the metro and about how computable that accessibility information is. Our study is based on the information obtained from the official metro websites of several European cities (see TABLE I).

TABLE I Summary of linked open data and accessibility information in European cities' metro transport media

European city	5-star classification	Accessibility information
Barcelona	***	×
Berlin	*	×
Hamburg	*	√
Istanbul	*	√
London	**	√
Madrid	*	√
Milan	*	√
Moscow	***	×
Munich	*	√
Oslo	*	×
Paris	*	×
Rome	*	√
Saint Petersburg	*	√
Vienna	*	×

We have focused on the fourteen cities, which have the largest metro networks -in kilometers-. These cities are, in alphabetical order: Barcelona, Berlin, Hamburg, Istanbul, London, Madrid, Milan, Moscow, Munich, Oslo, Paris, Rome, Saint Petersburg and Vienna. We have then analyzed how open, linked and computable the data on the websites are, that is, how many stars they have attained in the *linked open data 5-star* classification of Tim Berners-Lee [22]. To finish, we have checked, for each city, whether accessibility data exists on the website. We concluded that:

a) no city has four or five stars for the data shown on its website, that is, there is no linked open data on the metro companies' official websites;

b) 10/14 cities provide open data of the lowest category (the one-star category);

c) 3/14 cities only provide data as regards the three star category;

d) 8/14 cities show transport media accessibility.

It is, therefore, possible to conclude that it is not easy to find relevant information about public transport accessibility on the Internet.

B. Accessibility information of GTFS

GTFS [4] is a format for public transportation schedules and associated geographic information. A feed of GTFS is a collection of a maximum of six CSV files, with a .txt extension. Only two of these files currently include some sort of information regarding accessibility and special needs: *stops.txt* and *trips.txt*.

With regard to the *stops.txt* file, GTFS states that "A stop is a location where vehicles stop to pick up or drop off passengers. Stops can be grouped together, such as when there are multiple stops within a single station. This is done by defining one stop for the station, and defining it as a parent for all the stops it contains. Stops may also have zone identifiers, to group them together into zones". The *stops.txt* file includes an optional column denominated as wheelchair_boarding to indicate accessibility to this kind of information about a stop. GTFS states that "It identifies whether wheelchair boardings are possible from the specified stop or station."

With regard to the *trips.txt* file, GTFS states that "A trip represents a journey taken by a vehicle through stops. So, a single trip represents one journey along a transit line or route". This file includes two columns, both optional, related to accessibility limitations or special needs: wheelchair_accessible and bikes_allowed. In this work, we address only accessibility aspects and will not, therefore, discuss the bikes_allowed field.

In both files, the accessibility information provided by GTFS refers only to mobility impairment, while other impairment characteristics have not been considered: the special needs of deaf and blind people. In a previous work, we proposed to enhance accessibility information in Google Maps by adding new pieces of information to GTFS [23].

V. Our Proposal

The intent of our proposal is to improve accessibility information in order to support new social accessibility services, such as calculating public transport routes that are accessible to all. The eventual objective is to provide datasets as open data so as to support these services.

We work with the Identification of Fixed Objects in Public Transport (IFOPT [15]) reference datamodel. It is a prCEN ("Comité Européen de Normalisation –CEN-" in French) Technical Specification and, as mentioned previously, defines a model (and also the identification principles) for the main fixed objects related to public access to Public Transport (e.g., stop points, stop areas, stations, connection links, entrances, etc.). It already includes specific structures with which to describe accessibility data concerning the equipment of vehicles, stops and access areas.

In this work, we describe the process defined in order to generate a public transport dataset from public transport data and to make it accessible. This process consists of the following steps:

1. Study the accessibility features of the public transport network included on the official website of the transport media.
2. Identify the data semantics of this accessibility information in order to align them with a reference vocabulary (MAnto [24]);
3. If the alignment is possible, obtain the original data and semantically annotate them; if the alignment is not possible, analyze the difference between the original data and the reference vocabulary in order to extend it and, in this case, return to the second step;
4. Use the dataset as a service to improve the lives of citizens and public transport users.

In the following subsection, we validate the process against real data for the subway in the city of Madrid, Spain (Metro Madrid [2]).

A. *A case study: Collecting and annotating data concerning Metro Madrid in Spain*

In order to carry out the case study, it was necessary to use real data concerning Metro Madrid. We applied the four steps defined in the aforementioned process:

- First, we studied the lines, the stations on each line and the accessibility features. Metro Madrid specifies accessibility in two different ways. The first is on the *stations* webpage, where the user can determine whether a station is accessible and the kind of accessibility (universal or partial). The second is on the specific *accessible stations* webpage, where the user can determine the kind of accessibility of each station (universal or partial). More information on this website can be found in [5].
- Second, we identified the data semantics of the Metro Madrid accessibility features so as to align them with MAnto. TABLE II shows the correspondence between both.

TABLE II RELATIONSHIP BETWEEN METRO MADRID ACCESSIBILITY AND MANTO.

Accessibility stations and quays - Metro Madrid-	Accessibility Limitations -MAnto-
Universal accessibility	WheelchairAccess *true* AudibleSignsAvailable *true* StepFreeAccess *unknown* LiftFreeAccess *false* EscalatorFreeAccess *unknown* VisualSignsAvailable *true*
Complementary accessibility measures without lifts and/or ramps	WheelchairAccess *false* AudibleSignsAvailable *true* StepFreeAccess *unknown* LiftFreeAccess *true* EscalatorFreeAccess *unknown* VisualSignsAvailable *true*
Lifts and/or ramps without complementary accessibility measures	WheelchairAccess *true* AudibleSignsAvailable *false* StepFreeAccess *unknown* LiftFreeAccess *false* EscalatorFreeAccess *unknown* VisualSignsAvailable *false*

- Third, as Metro Madrid does not provide the means required to download these data, we developed a scraper to determine which stations are accessible and their kind of accessibility in each case. This information was semantically annotated and stored in RDF/XML (Resource Description Framework/eXtensible Markup Language) [25]. The accessibility information concerning Metro Madrid is specified at quay level. Each stop place has two quays. For example, at the Sol stop place, only quay 2 on line 1 is not accessible for wheelchairs, as is shown in Figure 2.

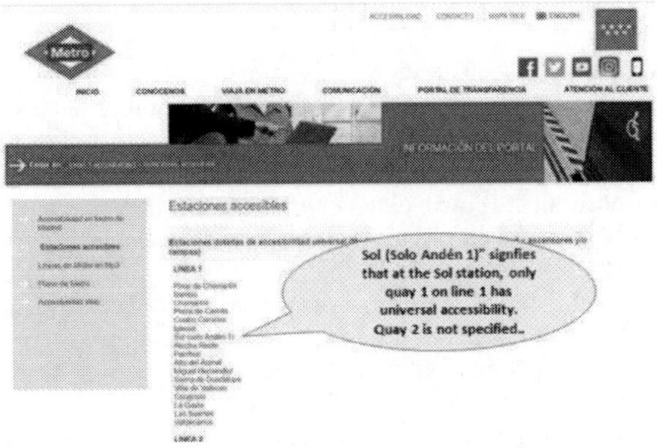

Figure 2 Quay 2 on line 1 is not accessible for wheelchairs at the Sol stop place.

The following piece of the code describes the accessibility for Metro Madrid, focusing on the Sol stop place and the two quays on lines number 1 and 2 (see Figure 3).

```
@prefix rdf: <http://www.w3.org/1999/02/22-rdf-syntax-
  ns#>.
@prefix mao: <com.vortic3.MANTO#>.

mao:StopPlace_Sol rdf:type mao:StopPlace ;
 mao:StopPlaceName "Sol" ;
 mao:StopPlace_Quay_has mao:Quay011 ;
 mao:StopPlace_Quay_has mao:Quay012 ;
 mao:StopPlace_Quay_has mao:Quay021 ;
 mao:StopPlace_Quay_has mao:Quay022 .

mao:Quay011 rdf:type mao:Quay ;
 mao:QuayName "Line1Quay1" ;
 mao:AccessibilityLimitation_WheelchairAccess "true";
 mao:AccessibilityLimitation_AudibleSignsAvailable
  "true";
 mao:AccessibilityLimitation_StepFreeAccess "unknown";
 mao:AccessibilityLimitation_LiftFreeAccess "false";
 mao:AccessibilityLimitation_EscalatorFreeAccess
  "unknown";
 mao:AccessibilityLimitation_VisualSignsAvailable "true".

mao:Quay012 rdf:type mao:Quay ;
 mao:QuayName "Line1Quay2" ;
 mao:AccessibilityLimitation_WheelchairAccess "false";
 mao:AccessibilityLimitation_AudibleSignsAvailable
  "true";
 mao:AccessibilityLimitation_StepFreeAccess "unknown";
 mao:AccessibilityLimitation_LiftFreeAccess "false";
 mao:AccessibilityLimitation_EscalatorFreeAccess
  "unknown";
 mao:AccessibilityLimitation_VisualSignsAvailable "true".

mao:Quay021 rdf:type mao:Quay ;
 mao:QuayName "Line2Quay1" ;
 mao:AccessibilityLimitation_WheelchairAccess "true" ;
 mao:AccessibilityLimitation_AudibleSignsAvailable"true";
 mao:AccessibilityLimitation_StepFreeAccess "unknown";
 mao:AccessibilityLimitation_LiftFreeAccess "false";
 mao:AccessibilityLimitation_EscalatorFreeAccess
  "unknown";
 mao:AccessibilityLimitation_VisualSignsAvailable "true".

mao:Quay022  rdf:type mao:Quay ;
 mao:QuayName "Line2Quay2" ;
 mao:AccessibilityLimitation_WheelchairAccess "true" ;
 mao:AccessibilityLimitation_AudibleSignsAvailable
  "true";
 mao:AccessibilityLimitation_StepFreeAccess "unknown";
 mao:AccessibilityLimitation_LiftFreeAccess "false";
 mao:AccessibilityLimitation_EscalatorFreeAccess
  "unknown";
 mao:AccessibilityLimitation_VisualSignsAvailable "true".
```

Figure 3 Accessibility of Metro Madrid by means of MAnto.

- Fourth, the dataset was used in the Android prototype app. It makes possible for users to obtain an accessible route on the metro by means of a specific algorithm, taking into account their different needs. Perhaps no accessible route exists, but if one does, then this app will be able to calculate it. The user interface in Figure 4a shows the information the prototype requires in order to establish the route: first, the origin and the destination of the route; second, the list of user's special needs (people with special mobility needs, blind people, hearing-impaired people), and third, the characteristics of the route (minimizing commutes or stations). The list of special needs is related to the columns in TABLE II. As previously mentioned, the first column identifies universal accessibility (everyone can travel), no lifts or ramps (blind and hearing-impaired people can travel, but mobility impaired people cannot), and only lifts and ramps (people with special mobility needs can travel, but blind or deaf people cannot).

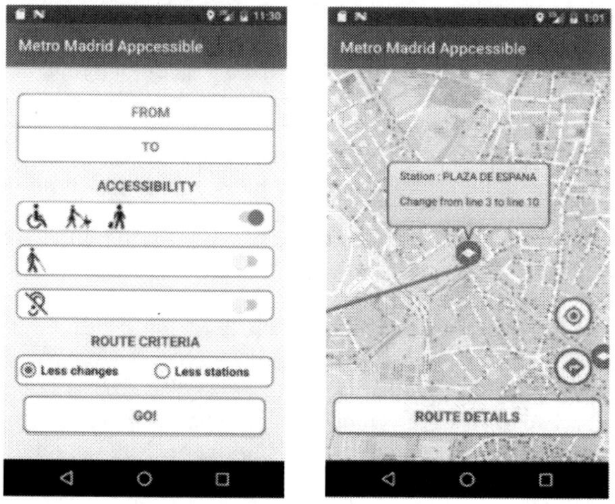

Figure 4 (a) App user interface requesting user needs; (b) Calculated accessible route.

Such accessibility features must match the special needs as shown in the prototype app. An example of an accessible route (for people with special mobility needs) is also shown in Figure 4b.

We have to underline that the app is just a prototype. A prototype because it does not include: (1) an accessible user interface; (2) downloading live updates or incident locations in the Metro Madrid network; (3) uploading updates or incidents identified by the user of the app.

The purpose of this prototype is to generate subway routes from the Metro Madrid data according to the specific user's needs; in this way, it includes: (a) a user interface in which a user can select his/her user's needs (only those that the Metro Madrid data can support); (b) the generation of accessible subway routes from the origin to a destination according to the user's needs.

With regard to the validation of the app, we have tested that the generated routes are effectively correct (verified in real-life), that is, that the routes can be used by people with specific disabilities identified in the user's needs.

VI. CONCLUSION AND FUTURE WORK

One of the major goals of smart cities is to achieve an inclusive society through the use of technologies. In this context, one important challenge is to facilitate the mobility of all citizens. If this challenge is to be met, information regarding means of transport and their accessibility features is, therefore, required in order to be able to provide accessible routes for every user, including special needs users.

As shown in this paper, these accessibility data are not easy to find and cannot be processed owing to the diversity of sources and formats. We have presented a study of the state of accessibility data in several European cities and shown that GTFS does not provide the constructions required to represent accessibility data. In order to resolve this issue, we have proposed a systematic process with which to gather the information, unify the formats and semantically annotate it: the first step is carried out by means of a scrapper; in the second and the third steps, we represent the data in RDF so as to unify and annotate the data for their further use in applications that help citizens move in a city.

As future work, we intend to improve the systematic process defined in this work in order to provide fully open datasets of different public transport networks. Moreover, these datasets must be published in an open platform that will permit free access to accessibility and special needs data. The process will take into account the accessible routes generated using crowdsourcing techniques. These routes will be generated by users with special needs. We have to developed different apps for these kinds of users with the aim of capturing the geographical information and the accessibility characteristics of these routes. This information will be incorporated as smart data into the Multiply@City platform (see Figure 1). Moreover, the apps still have to be validated and will be developed following the existing standards and initiatives of accessible user interfaces. The same directives have to be applied to the protoype app presented in this paper.

ACKNOWLEDGMENT

This work is supported by the Multiply@City project (TIN2016-78103-C2-1-R) and the Access@City project (TIN2016-78103-C2-1-R), funded by the Spanish Ministry of Economy and Competitiveness.

We would like to thank Miguel Maroto for his support.

REFERENCES

[1] The Global Initiatives for ICTs (G3ict), http://g3ict.org/resource_center/g3ict_smart_cities_initiative, [retrieved: March, 2018].

[2] World ENABLED, http://worldenabled.org, [retrieved: March, 2018].

[3] Smart Cities for All, a Global Strategy for Digital Inclusion proposed by G3ict and World ENABLED, March 2017.

[4] Google Transit Feed Specification, https://developers.google.com/transit/gtfs/, [retrieved: March, 2018].

[5] Metro MADRID, http://www.metromadrid.es/en/, [retrieved: March, 2018].

[6] NAPTAN, http://transport.data.gov.uk/def/naptan [retrieved: March, 2018].

[7] Ofi-ontology, http://ip-kom.net/data/html_documentation_ontologien/ofi-ontology.html [retrieved: March, 2018].

[8] DBpedia,http://mappings.dbpedia.org/index.php/OntologyProperty:IsHandicappedAccessible, [retrieved: March, 2018].

[9] TubeFacility, https://github.com/AccessAtECS/RailGB/blob/master/standard/public/ajax/tube.php [retrieved: March, 2018].

[10] Accessibility ontology, https://github.com/ox-it/accessibility-ontology/blob/master/accessibility-ontology.ttl [retrieved: March, 2018].

[11] TRANSIT, http://vocab.org/transit, [retrieved: March, 2018].

[12] T. Sarjakoski, P. Kettunen,H. Halkosaari, M. Laakso, M. Rönneberg, H. Stigmar, Landmarks and a Hiking Ontology to Support Wayfinding in a National Park During Different Seasons. In M. Raubal, D. M. Mark, and A. U. Frank (Eds.), Cognitive and Linguistic Aspects of Geographic Space, Lecture Notes in Geoinformation and Cartography. Berlin, Heidelberg: Springer Berlin Heidelberg, 2013. DOI:10.1007/978-3-642-34359-9.

[13] OASIS, http://www.oasis-project.eu/ [retrieved: March, 2018].

[14] Transmodel, standardization, E. C. (2016). Transmodel, Road Transport and Traffic Telematics. Public Transport. Ref. Data Model, EN 12896, http://www.transmodel.org/en/cadre1.html, [retrieved: March, 2018].

[15] CEN/TC 278. Intelligent transport systems - Public transport - Identification of Fixed Objects In Public Transport (IFOPT), EN 28701:2012.

[16] C. E. Cuesta, P. Cáceres, B. Vela, and J. M. Cavero, "CoMobility: A Mobile Platform for Transport Sharing", ERCIM News 2013(93), pp. 22-23, 2013.

[17] Access@City project (TIN2016-78103-C2-1-R), funded by the Spanish Ministry of Economy and Competitiveness.

[18] Multiply@City project (TIN2016-78103-C2-1-R), funded by the Spanish Ministry of Economy and Competitiveness.

[19] Regional Consortium for Public Transports of Madrid (CRTM), http://datos.crtm.es/, [retrieved: March, 2018].

[20] EMT Madrid home page, http://www.emtmadrid.es/Index.aspx?lang=en-GB, [retrieved: March, 2018].

[21] Spanish National Society of Blind People (ONCE, Organización Nacional de Ciegos de España) http://www.once.es/new/otras-webs/english, [retrieved: March, 2018].

[22] 5-star classification, Tim Berners-Lee, http://5stardata.info/en/, [retrieved: March, 2018].

[23] P. Cáceres, A. Sierra-Alonso, C. E. Cuesta, J. M. Cavero, and B. Vela, "Enhancing Accessibility Information in Google Maps: Adding new pieces of information to GTFS to improve accessibility" In Proceedings on the Second International Conference on Universal Accessibility in the Internet of Things and Smart Environments (SMART ACCESSIBILITY), pp. 6-9, Nice (France), 2017.

[24] Mobility and Accessibility Ontology (MAnto): https://vortic3.github.io/MANTO/, [retrieved: March, 2018].

[25] RDF/XML (Resource Description Framework/eXtensible Markup Language), https://www.w3.org/TR/rdf-syntax-grammar/, [retrieved: March, 2018].

Monitoring a Grid of Sensors by Performance Metrics for Internet of Things Applications

Carolina Del-Valle-Soto, Jafet Rodriguez
Universidad Panamericana, Facultad de Ingenieria,
Jalisco, Mexico.
Email: cvalle@up.edu.mx, arodrig@up.edu.mx

Carlos Mex-Perera
ITAM,
Ciudad de Mexico, Mexico
Email: jorge.mex@itam.mx

***Abstract*—A sensor network is composed of nodes which collaborate in a common task. These nodes have certain sensory capabilities and wireless communication that allow forming ad-hoc networks, i.e., no pre-established physical structure or central administration is necessary. Therefore, one of the main problems with ad-hoc systems is that there is no existing infrastructure, so the routes change dynamically. This is due to fading, interference, disconnection of nodes, obstacles, node movements, and so on. We expose an analysis of the Multi-Parent Hierarchical (MPH) routing protocol for wireless sensor networks, which has low overhead, reduced latency and low energy consumption. Network performance simulations of the MPH routing protocol are carried out and compared with two popular protocols, Ad-hoc On-Demand Distance Vector (AODV), Dynamic Source Routing (DSR) and the well-known algorithm Zigbee Tree Routing (ZTR). The combination of a hierarchical topology with self-configuration and maintenance mechanisms of the MPH protocol makes nodes optimize network processes, reduce delays, take short routes to the destination and decrease network overhead. All this is reflected in the successful delivery of information.**

Keywords–Wireless Sensor Networks; Energy Consumption; Performance Metrics; Routing Protocol; Internet of Things.

I. INTRODUCTION

Wireless Sensor Networks (WSNs) are based on low-cost devices (nodes) that are able to get information from their environment, process it locally, and communicate via wireless links to a central coordinator node. Additionally, the coordinator node might also send control commands to the nodes [1]. WSNs may not rely on a predetermined structure and require the capacity of self-organization in order to deal with communications impairments, mobility and node failures. Moreover, it is important to study the scalability and adaptation methods of the network in the face of topology changes and packet transmission failures in the wireless medium.

In this work, scenarios of wireless sensor networks are proposed under different configurations of topology arrays. The aim is to contrast the performance of the sensor network under three widely known protocols in the literature: AODV [2], DSR [3] and MPH [4]. The latter was designed and implemented by the same authors of this work in the reference cited in [4]. In this study, AODV, DSR, ZTR [5] and MPH are compared based on various efficiency metrics and how they optimize routing protocols through energy. There are several schemes to find the best routes in the shortest possible time. In terms of hierarchy algorithms, such as ZTR, it has a simple and fast routing, which reduces overload in the network, is reliable and has a distributed addressing scheme that does not require nodes to have routing tables. Results from our work show that for the single sink scenario, the MPH protocol has an energy saving of 35% against AODV and DSR protocols and 8% compared with ZTR. MPH has 27% less overhead compared with AODV and DSR. Moreover, MPH presents a 10% increase in packet delivery compared with AODV, DSR and ZTR.

We describe the organization of the rest of the paper. Section 2 introduces the related work on the wireless sensor network problem to an IoT approach. Section 3 proposes the analysis of performance metrics. Section 4 describes and explains the analysis of performance metrics under a grid topology. Furthermore, Section 5 presents the results. Section 6 has the study of sensors as base of Internet of Things. Finally, conclusions are given in Section 7.

II. RELATED WORK

Due to technological advancements, the Internet is being used to share data among different small, resource-constrained devices connected in number of billions to constitute the Internet of Things (IoT). A large amount of data from these devices imposes overhead on the IoT network. Hence, it is required to provide solutions for various network related problems in IoT including routing, energy conservation, congestion, heterogeneity, scalability, reliability, quality of service (QoS) and security to optimally make use of the available network.

One of the most efficient topologies in information delivery is the hierarchical topology [6]. The hierarchy levels allow packet forwarding with the least number of hops, which causes fewer errors in delivery and lower delays in the transmission of a packet from source to destination. Hierarchical protocols have scalability and robustness characteristics, providing energy savings in the network and distributing energy costs among network sensors. A great advantage of such protocols is that they carry information generally to one node, thus the communication with the coordinator or root node is simpler and more efficient [7]. Tree Routing is a classic form of routing that is restricted to parent-child links. This scheme eliminates the need for searching and updating paths and the overhead associated with the establishment of those paths. However, when the networks are large and the nodes can connect and disconnect from the network due to link changing conditions, it is helpful for the Tree Routing scheme to be able to change slightly, offering more flexibility in assigning IP addresses to the network in order to become self-organized because it is performed using fewer links. In addition, the hierarchical protocols have simple routing algorithms that guarantee efficient delivery of information and increase the lifetime of the network.

A reliable routing protocol in WSNs is essential due to the versatility of these networks. In [8], the authors analyze metrics such as end-to-end path reliability and number of hops. Their work analyzes different routing algorithms based on link reliability models for each type of node. In [9], a routing protocol that guarantees the route with the shortest path while maintaining Quality of Service is designed. The route optimization is related to the ideal relay node position and metrics such as mean end-to-end delay and packet rate under random scenarios are considered [10]. The influence of packet retransmissions in communication and its effects on energy efficiency in the network are analyzed. Some of the most adaptable protocols for this type of networks are AODV and DSR, which are aimed at reducing cost and energy consumption and improving reliability. These protocols allow multi-hopping among the actively involved nodes that want to establish and maintain routes in a network [11]. On the other hand, ZTR, a widely referenced algorithm, has low overhead and is simple with regard to the memory capacity of the nodes since they do not have routing tables, which eliminates path searching and updating. Nevertheless, it has some drawbacks in terms of flexibility and adaptation, especially when it is deployed in wide network environments [5].

III. Performance Metrics

Metrics of the network layer are very important because they show the performance and usefulness of a routing protocol. Each routing protocol is designed for specific applications and certain scenarios. These metrics indicate how the use of bandwidth is affected by the overhead of the routing protocol in use. In addition, the availability of effective routes and the ability of the network for self-configuration show the capacity of the protocol to recover from topology changes. Recovery times have an impact on the latency in the network and even though the networks conform with different technologies, it is highly important to understand and evaluate the performance metrics as shown in [12].

A. Optimization of Routes

An important feature in a sensor network is when nodes lose established routes due to mobility or changes in the topology. It is necessary to have a protocol that can find optimal routes and can adapt to network changes. Applications of sensor networks were used by such and such authors to conduct a study about Energy Optimal Routing algorithm in [13] for mining and tunneling approaches, which is very significant in energy savings in sensors due to their long time period in harsh environments unsuitable for constant human access. This algorithm builds routes based on transmission distance and search optimization. Moreover, it employs energy balancing strategy. In [14] Nezhad et al. proposed a Destination Controlled Anonymous Routing Protocol for Sensornets routing protocol for high traffic sensor networks. In this work, the authors propose a collector node capable of having a global view of the whole network topology representing a higher level of hierarchy than the other nodes. In [15], Nasser et al. proposed the Secure and Energy-Efficient multipath Routing protocol that combines multi-path technique for communication among nodes, as well as safety techniques with respect to malicious attacks to a destination. This protocol is proposed for an environment of static nodes. It stores information in the node routing tables with the routes to a collector node as a final destination. This contributes to a new proposal for the establishment and maintenance of routes.

B. Routing Protocols in WSNs

In communication networks, there are routing protocols classified into two groups: proactive routing protocols and reactive routing protocols. When nodes are under a reactive protocol, they ask for a route only when it is needed. This involves high latency for the first packet and some independence among routes. The AODV routing protocol is based on routing efficiency of wireless ad-hoc networks with a huge number of nodes and it uses a route discovery mechanism in broadcast mode. It is considered as a reactive protocol: the routes are created only when they are needed, on demand. AODV can transmit in unicast or multicast mode. It uses the bandwidth efficiently and responds to the network changes in a very quick mode, preventing network loops [2]. In fact, AODV maintains time-based states in the routing tables of each node. An entry in the routing table expires if it has not been used recently. The timer function is designed to avoid the use of links which the node does not have an updated status from a long time ago. Some advantages of AODV include more reliability and less cost in bandwidth. However, there are some disadvantages, as follows: more complexity and computing, more cost in memory, and this protocol was designed to work in a network where there are no malicious nodes. In conclusion, it is not a secure protocol.

The DSR protocol is a reactive protocol. It routes from source node including a header in the packets. It indicates what nodes will be crossed to arrive at a destination because the origin node is responsible for calculating the complete path to the destination node. This process is called *Source Routing*. Each node in the network has a cache memory which stores all of the obtained routes throughout discovery processes, this could be from the source node or learned from the network. If there is no current route to a specific destination, the node begins a *Route Discovery*. The route table or route cache is constantly monitored to detect broken or invalid routes, in order to repair them, when the network topology has changed. This process is called *Route Maintenance*. DSR protocol presents some advantages; for instance, a node can obtain multiple paths to a specific destination by only requesting for a route. Also, it allows the network to be entirely self-configuring without a particular architecture or topology. Additionally, it is a good election in scenarios where the number of mobile nodes is limited. Furthermore, the protocol adapts itself quickly to routing changes when a node is frequently moving, and finally, this protocol decreases the overhead in the network.

ZTR is a simple protocol which establishes parent-child links and the nodes always carry information to their parent. It has a tree topology and is easy to implement. ZigBee requires that there is at least one full-function device with a more robust nature to act as a network coordinator, but the final nodes can have reduced function in order to reduce costs. The parent node is the one which has given the child access to the network, so parent-child links are created, but each child can only have one parent. Some of the advantages of ZTR are that in the algorithm implemented in the network layer, there is a balance between cost per unit, battery expense, complexity of implementation to achieve a proper cost-performance relation to the application.

MPH creates a hierarchical network logical topology where the hierarchy of the nodes is given by its location level, which is proactive. It works like a hierarchical tree: nodes establish parent and child links that constitute the possible routes. Node hierarchies are used to establish links between parents and children based on the coverage radius that depends on the transmission power. As a result, a node can share both the children and the parents with another node belonging to the same hierarchical level, which allows more links, but does not generate unnecessary routes, and continues to express speed thanks to the hierarchical topology. This protocol takes advantage of the controlled maintenance of routes of the proactive nature, but combines the agility that allows to have more than one route for a node. This makes it more versatile and adaptable to different topologies.

IV. Analysis of Performance Metrics Under a Grid Topology

WSNs consist of a number of spatially distributed autonomous devices using sensors to monitor physical or environmental conditions. They are multi-functional, low-cost and low-power networks, and rely on communications among nodes or from sensor nodes to one or more sink nodes. Sink nodes, sometimes called coordinator nodes or root nodes, may be more robust and have larger processing capacity than the other nodes. Sensor networks can be widely used in various environments, sometimes hostile. Some of the many applications of WSNs are in the medical field, agriculture, monitoring and detection, automation and data mining.

The most notable issues regarding WSNs are the difficulty in transmitting information in a wireless environment as well as the energy costs implied. When the signal suffers from physical obstacles, channel occupancy, interference and general fading with other devices, it promotes the use of high energy consuming mechanisms to send and receive packets successfully. These networks have limited resources because of the cost and size of the devices. The sensors are small in order to be adaptable to all kinds of environments and able to be installed in various conditions, locations, and infrastructures. This also causes the batteries to be small and short-lived; thus creating the need to save energy in all processes of the network.

We take into account performance metrics that directly or indirectly influence the energy consumption of a network. The delay may be an indication that packets are not directed on the optimal path, which shows an increase in the number of hops to reach the final destination. When routes are not optimal this brings more energy consumption. When the number of retransmissions is high this may be a consequence of the large number of collisions that are in the channel, and nodes can be strained to bring the information to its destination. The connections and disconnections of nodes make the network topology change constantly. This is why the implemented routing protocol must be able to respond quickly and efficiently to these failures. The availability of routes is a parameter showing the capacity of the routing protocol to maintain current valid routes due to the fact that nodes are constantly asking for routes, increasing the overhead.

V. Results

In this section, we compare the performance of the MPH protocol with that of commonly used protocols in sensor networks, such as AODV, DSR and the well-known algorithm, ZTR. We consider the following important metrics that are indicative of network performance and they are tested under the topology described in Figure 1.

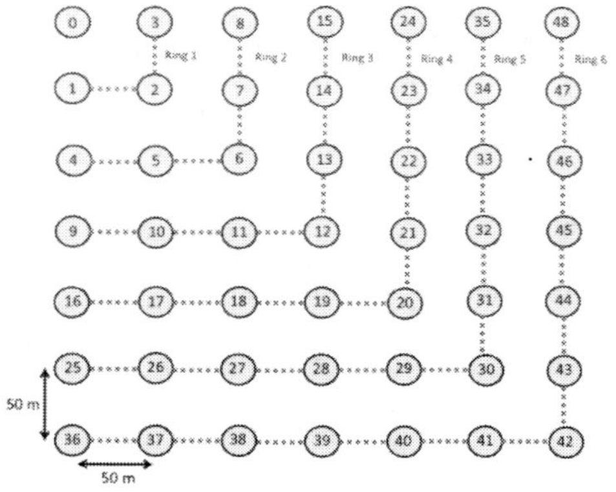

Figure 1. Network topology.

Table I describes the parameters of the simulations.

TABLE I. SIMULATION AND REAL NETWORK PARAMETERS. CARRIER SENSE MULTIPLE ACCESS WITH COLLISION AVOIDANCE (CSMA/CA) [16].

Parameter	**Value**
Physical Layer Parameters	
Sensitivity threshold receiver	−94 dBm
Transmission power	4.5 dBm
MAC Layer Parameters	
Maximum retransmission number	3
Maximum retry number	5
Maximum number of tries to reach a node from the collector	9
Packet error rate	1%
Average frame length	22 bytes
Maximum number of backoffs	4
MAC protocol	IEEE 802.15.4
MAC layer	CSMA/CA
Network Layer Parameters	
Number of nodes	49
Maximum data rate	250 kbps
Scenario	Static nodes

1) Delay: The time a packet takes to reach its destination is variable due to several factors, for instance: the transmission speed, the packet size and the delay of the packet in each hop in the route. Collisions and packet retransmissions also increase the end-to-end delay. The delay is related to the network complexity. The MPH protocol, through the election of a hierarchical topology, produces a reduction of the delays in the information delivery process.

It is important to consider the delay involved in reorganizing the network due to changes in connectivity, for example, due to new nodes or nodes that switch off or are faulty. Table II shows relevant delays obtained in the simulations of the

MPH protocol compared with AODV, DSR, and ZTR. The first row shows the time required to complete the process of table maintenance performed by a neighbor node. With this process, each node builds its neighbor table. The second row describes the time it takes a packet to travel from the farthest node to the coordinator (these are the nodes of the last ring shown in Figure 1). In the third row, we obtained the time it takes a packet from the nearest ring in Figure 1 (one hop) to get to its destination, for each of the protocols. In the fourth, fifth, sixth, seventh and eighth rows, we randomly turned off 10%, 20%, 30%, 40% and 50% of the network nodes, respectively. We observed how long it takes a packet to reach the coordinator node from the farthest node in the topology. In the ninth row, we define the recovery time for the worst case (50% nodes turned off). This metric takes into account the self-configuring time of the network due to the dynamics of the wireless scenario, such as node disconnections. This is where we see the ability of each routing protocol to overcome topology changes and reorganize the network.

2) Energy consumption: The energy model implemented for the three protocols studied is presented in Table III. When MPH is used, nodes store neighbor tables, and routing is done via the optimal route. Therefore, this protocol provides large energy savings thanks to multi-parent routes. This can be seen in Figure 2a, where we observe that AODV and DSR use more total energy than MPH because they require more routing overhead, which causes more collisions and retransmissions. ZTR does not carry out a discovery mechanism but it has less available links and does not guarantee that those are the shortest routes, so, sometimes it needs more hops.

3) Overhead: Reactive protocols such as AODV and DSR have low overhead because routes are discovered only when they are needed. However, MPH and ZTR use fewer control packets, thus nodes have low processing and simple management of neighbor tables. Therefore, MPH maintains neighbor tables with fewer control packets. ZTR does not need to maintain any table. This behavior can be seen in Figure 2b.

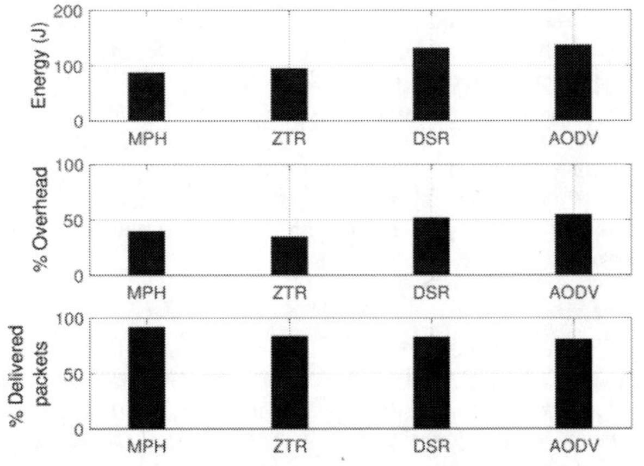

Figure 2. (a) Total energy, (b) Overhead, (c) Packet delivery ratio.

4) Packet delivery ratio: We took a radius of 10 m and analyzed the percentage of delivered packets for AODV, DSR, ZTR and MPH. The value that this metric takes is a consequence of the ability of a routing protocol to reorganize the network. Besides, if the number of hops the packets pass through is smaller, there will be fewer errors in the information delivery. Results are depicted in Figure 2c.

VI. SENSORS AS BASE OF INTERNET OF THINGS

Internet of Things (IoT) [17]] allows the possibility of digital interaction among objects, through the Internet, without the intervention of human beings. Thanks to wireless systems, it is possible to integrate a chip of a few millimeters in any object in the home, work or city to process and transmit information from it constantly. One of the biggest challenges of IoT is to have real-time data that are visible to extract valuable information. The goal is to have accurate information to make better decisions by discovering which data is essential through intelligent filtering. In addition, it allows understanding the signals within the data. Thus, organizations can extract and analyze data through the connected IoT ecosystem [18].

Internet of Things is precisely one of the leading areas where sensors have a fundamental role since they are the instruments capable of gathering weather, traffic, electricity, gas and water data and combine it with real-time images to understand how a neighborhood behaves. In other words, the sensors are aware of all the digital pulses in each activity in a city.

1) Availability of routes: Reliable or valid routes are the routes that are active and can be used by nodes to send packets. These routes may expire (according to the routing protocol) or may disappear from the tables due to disconnections of neighbor nodes. The most reliable routes will ensure more reliable delivery of information.

We turned off a certain percentage of network nodes to observe nodes disconnections. In this way, we could see how some routes become invalid and how nodes respond to reconfigure valid routes in the network, depending on the protocol. The percentage of reliable routes is presented in Figure 3.

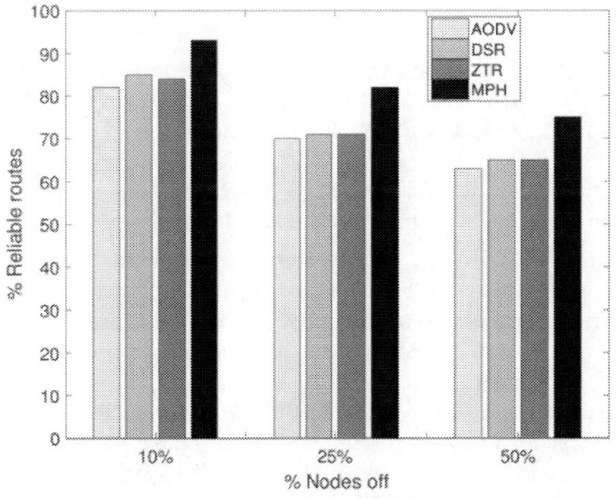

Figure 3. % Nodes off vs % Reliable routes.

Due to the persistence mechanism in MPH, that is a parameter that makes a soft output from the neighbor tables,

TABLE II. DELAY.

PARAMETER	AODV	DSR	ZTR	MPH
Neighbor discovery process for an average of 8 neighbors.	32.672 ms	31.592 ms	16.243 ms	29.924 ms
Average time it takes a traffic packet to reach its destination without shutdown nodes in the network (ring farthest to destination).	152.671 ms	142.411 ms	63.141 ms	62.393 ms
Average time it takes a traffic packet to reach its destination without shutdown nodes in the network (ring closest to destination).	11.937 ms	10.493 ms	10.723 ms	10.399 ms
Average time it takes a traffic packet to reach its destination with 10% shutdown nodes in the network (ring farthest to destination).	95.415 ms	93.245 ms	92.113 ms	85.836 ms
Average time it takes a traffic packet to reach its destination with 20% shutdown nodes in the network (ring farthest to destination).	97.428 ms	95.678 ms	92.436 ms	86.336 ms
Average time it takes a traffic packet to reach its destination with 30% shutdown nodes in the network (ring farthest to destination).	98.768 ms	98.258 ms	94.226 ms	88.126 ms
Average time it takes a traffic packet to reach its destination with 40% shutdown nodes in the network (ring farthest to destination).	100.258 ms	99.356 ms	96.116 ms	89.963 ms
Average time it takes a traffic packet to reach its destination with 50% shutdown nodes in the network (ring farthest to destination).	105.247 ms	104.385 ms	100.122 ms	92.836 ms
Recovery of topology with 50% shutdown nodes (the worst case).	34 sec	33 sec	21 sec	20 sec

TABLE III. ENERGY MODEL.

	Voltage (mV)	Current (mA)	Time (ms)
Start-up mode	120	12	0.2
MCU running on 32-MHz clock	75	7.5	1.7
CSMA/CA algorithm	270	27	1.068
Switch from RX to TX	140	14	0.2
Switch from TX to RX	250	25	0.2
Radio in RX mode (processing and waiting)	250	25	4.1915
Radio in TX mode	320	32	0.58
Shut down mode	75	7.5	2.5

TABLE IV. % VALID ROUTES.

TIME	% Valid Routes			
	AODV	DSR	ZTR	MPH
10	70	70	90	98
20	82	83	89	97
30	90	91	89	98
40	97	98	90	98
50	90	90	89	97
60	81	82	91	97
70	85	87	90	98
80	90	92	90	98
90	97	97	89	97
100	92	93	91	98

TABLE V. AVERAGE VALID ROUTES AND HOPS PER NODE.

TIME	AODV		DSR		ZTR		MPH	
	Routes	Hops	Routes	Hops	Routes	Hops	Routes	Hops
10	4.7	5	4.7	5	1	4.1	2.2	4.1
20	5.6	5	5.6	5	1	4.1	2.1	4.1
30	6.0	5	6.2	5	1	4.2	2.2	4.2
40	6.6	5	6.7	5	1	4.2	2.2	4.1
50	6.0	6	6.1	6	1	4.1	2.1	4.2
60	5.5	6	5.7	6	1	4.2	2.1	4.1
70	5.9	6	5.9	6	1	4.2	2.1	4.2
80	6.1	5	6.2	5	1	4.2	2.2	4.1
90	6.5	5	6.6	5	1	4.1	2.1	4.1
100	6.2	5	6.2	5	1	4.2	2.1	4.2

these become safer as well as more reliable, compared with AODV, DSR, and ZTR. This is so because in AODV routes have timers that expire after a certain period. On the other hand, DSR is aware that a route is obsolete only when it receives a route error message. ZTR does not have tables, so each time it needs to form the whole topology.

In Table IV, we took a sampling period of 100 seconds. We made tests every 10 seconds in which we compute the average number of valid routes available in case the node has to send a traffic packet right at this moment. In the AODV and DSR cases, occasionally some routes have just expired or some node in the route has been disconnected: these cases will result in invalid routes. In the ZTR case, sometimes, there is no route available to send the packet. On the other hand, when the MPH protocol is implemented, almost all the time the neighbor tables have valid routes ready to be used.

With regard to diversity of routes and hop count, we present Table V. The MPH protocol gets routes with a minimum number of hops but it has fewer routes. The advantage of MPH compared to the AODV and DSR protocols is that MPH does not require routing tables, the decision of a node to route a packet to the coordinator is very simple because a node chooses the most widely used route. In contrast, we see that AODV and DSR have more routes to the coordinator, but they do not always guarantee the shortest route. It is true that the node chooses the shortest route from its routing table but it may be that this route is not the shortest to the destination. This effect is due to the packet loss probability. Regarding ZTR, the route to the destination is unique because it does not have the multi-parent concept. This means that, if there is any disconnection of a node (or nodes), the probability of packet loss is higher, which is a big disadvantage. In this table, the number that shows the hops is an average number of the nodes every 10 seconds.

A. Retransmissions and retries

Figure 4 displays the average node retransmissions and the average CSMA/CA retries for the four studied protocols. Here, we remark that for the four protocols, initially, there are many retransmissions and CSMA/CA retries. This is so because, when the nodes connect to the network they begin by sending broadcast packets to discover neighbors, so there is a greater number of packets in the network: overhead and traffic packets produce more collisions. Note that in the retransmissions, during the first 10 seconds the four protocols increase their average amount of retransmissions(the line has the highest peak of the graph). This is because of the amount of packets flowing in the network during the time of formation of the topology. The CSMA retries also show this peak because as the channel is constantly busy, CSMA retries increase. However, regarding retransmissions, it is important to mention that this first peak has an average value of 2.7 for AODV and DSR, 2.6 for ZTR and 2.5 for MPH. Concerning also the first peak, the CSMA retries metric has an average value of 3.6 for AODV, 3.5 for DSR and ZTR and, 3.3 for MPH.

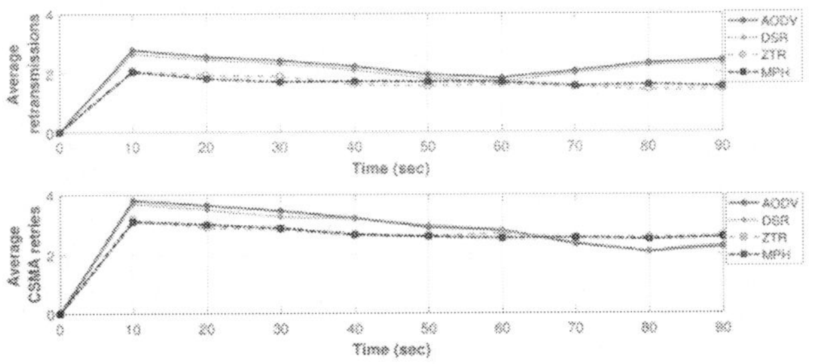

Figure 4. Time (sec) vs Average retransmissions and CSMA/CA retries.

VII. Conclusion

IoT enables physical devices or sensors to measure, perform a defined task, use the cloud for storage and to actuate the alert system automatically in case of an emergency situation with the aid of Internet as its underlying technology. Thus, IoT transforms these traditional devices to work in a smart way by using various deriving technologies such as pervasive computing, embedded devices, various communication standards and technologies.

In MPH, the coordinator node can be aware of approximately the whole topology due to the source routing mechanism. In AODV and DSR, the routes from the coordinator to some node are calculated the same way as the other routes. So, MPH has the advantage that the coordinator node can access any node to send information, statistics or measurements requests. In comparison with AODV and DSR, the coordinator has to discover the route to a specific node if it does not have it, which is not desirable. Also, MPH protocol has fewer control packets, therefore less overhead, resulting in fewer collisions, so there will be fewer packet retransmissions compared with AODV and DSR. Moreover, this is reflected in the energy saving metric. The ZTR algorithm does not present route diversity which enhances the probability of losing packets when there are disconnections of nodes.

The results for MPH protocol are encouraging because this protocol has good performance in terms of processing, fast and efficient information delivery and energy conservation. Protocols such as AODV and DSR are very efficient in terms of backup routes and connectivity from any node to any node in the network. ZTR is a simple and low energy cost algorithm, but it is not very reliable in adverse network conditions or failure on the links. The combination of a hierarchical topology with self-configuration and maintenance mechanisms of the MPH protocol makes the nodes optimize network processes, reduce delays, take short routes to the destination and decrease network overhead. All this is reflected in the successful delivery of information. As future work, this analysis of the performance of a sensor network should be complemented by low-power protocols on the Internet of things, such as 6LoWPAN (IPv6 over Low Power Wireless Personal Area Networks).

Acknowledgement

The author Carlos Mex-Perera has been supported by Asociación Mexicana de Cultura A.C.

References

[1] M. Aykut Yigitel, Ozlem Durmaz Incel, and Cem Ersoy, "QoS-aware MAC protocols for wireless sensor networks: A survey," Computer Networks, vol. 55, no. 8, 2011, pp. 1982 – 2004.

[2] C. E. Perkins and E. M. Royer, "Ad-hoc on-demand distance vector routing," in Proceedings - WMCSA'99: 2nd IEEE Workshop on Mobile Computing Systems and Applications, 1999, pp. 90–100.

[3] D. A. Maltz, J. Broch, J. Jetcheva, and D. B. Johnson, "Effects of on-demand behavior in routing protocols for multihop wireless ad hoc networks," IEEE Journal on Selected Areas in Communications, vol. 17, no. 8, 1999, pp. 1439–1453.

[4] C. Del-Valle Soto, C. Mex Perera, A. Orozco Lugo, G. M. Galvan Tejada, O. Olmedo, and M. Lara, "An efficient Multi-Parent Hierarchical routing protocol for WSNs," in Wireless Telecommunications Symposium, 2014.

[5] Z. Alliance, "ZigBee specification (document 053474r17)," vol. 21, 01 2008.

[6] J. Macker, "Mobile ad hoc networking (MANET): Routing protocol performance issues and evaluation considerations," 1999.

[7] C. Sergiou, V. Vassiliou, and A. Paphitis, "Hierarchical Tree Alternative Path (HTAP) algorithm for congestion control in wireless sensor networks," Ad Hoc Networks, vol. 11, no. 1, 2013, pp. 257–272.

[8] A. E. Zonouz, L. Xing, V. M. Vokkarane, and Y. L. Sun, "Reliability-oriented single-path routing protocols in wireless sensor networks," IEEE Sensors Journal, vol. 14, no. 11, 2014, pp. 4059–4068.

[9] A. Bhattacharya and A. Kumar, "A shortest path tree based algorithm for relay placement in a wireless sensor network and its performance analysis," Computer Networks, vol. 71, 2014, pp. 48–62.

[10] A. Kabila and A. Murugan, "Efficient Energy Performance of the Wireless Sensor Networks and Cross Layer Optimization," Asian Journal of Applied Science and Technology (AJAST), vol. 1, no. 3, 2017, pp. 55–58.

[11] J. Rahman, M. A. M. Hasan, and M. K. B. Islam, "Comparative analysis the performance of AODV, DSDV and DSR routing protocols in wireless sensor network," in 2012 7th International Conference on Electrical and Computer Engineering, ICECE 2012, 2012, pp. 283–286.

[12] S. Fauzia and K. Fatima, Performance evaluation of AODV routing protocol for free space optical mobile Ad-Hoc networks, ser. Advances in Intelligent Systems and Computing, 2018, vol. 683.

[13] H. Jiang, J. Qian, Y. Sun, and G. Zhang, "Energy optimal routing for long chain-type wireless sensor networks in underground mines," Mining Science and Technology, vol. 21, no. 1, 2011, pp. 17–21.

[14] A. A. Nezhad, A. Miri, and D. Makrakis, "Location privacy and anonymity preserving routing for wireless sensor networks," Computer Networks, vol. 52, no. 18, 2008, pp. 3433–3452.

[15] N. Nasser and Y. Chen, "SEEM: Secure and energy-efficient multipath routing protocol for wireless sensor networks," Computer Communications, vol. 30, no. 11-12, 2007, pp. 2401–2412.

[16] I. Computer Society, IEEE. Wireless medium access control (MAC) and physical layer (PHY) specifications for low-rate wireless personal area networks (WPANs). IEEE Standard 802.15.4-2006 (Revision of IEEE Standard 802.15.4-2003)., 2006, [retrieved: January, 2018].

[17] M. Sakamoto and T. Nakajima, "Some experiences with developing intelligent Internet-of-Things," in IEEE 2nd International Smart Cities Conference: Improving the Citizens Quality of Life, ISC2 2016 - Proceedings, 2016.

[18] S. Kurt, H. U. Yildiz, M. Yigit, B. Tavli, and V. C. Gungor, "Packet size optimization in wireless sensor networks for smart grid applications," IEEE Transactions on Industrial Electronics, vol. 64, no. 3, 2017, pp. 2392–2401.